INCARNATION

INCARNATION
REDISCOVERING THE SIGNIFICANCE OF CHRISTMAS

Incarnation: Rediscovering the Significance of Christmas
978-1-7910-1641-8
978-1-7910-0555-9 *eBook*
978-1-7910-0556-6 *Large Print*

Incarnation: DVD
978-1-7910-0559-7

Incarnation: Leader Guide
978-1-7910-0557-3
978-1-7910-0558-0 *eBook*

Incarnation: Youth Study Book
978-1-7910-0564-1
978-1-7910-0565-8 *eBook*

**Incarnation:
Children's Leader Guide**
978-1-7910-0553-5

Also by Adam Hamilton

24 Hours That Changed the World

Christianity and World Religions

Christianity's Family Tree

Confronting the Controversies

Creed

Enough

Faithful

Final Words from the Cross

Forgiveness

Half Truths

John

Leading Beyond the Walls

Love to Stay

Making Sense of the Bible

Moses

Not a Silent Night

Revival

*Seeing Gray in a World
of Black and White*

Selling Swimsuits in the Arctic

Simon Peter

Speaking Well

The Call

The Journey

The Walk

The Way

Unafraid

Unleashing the Word

When Christians Get It Wrong

Why?

For more information, visit www.AdamHamilton.com.

ADAM HAMILTON

Author of *The Journey, Not a Silent Night,* and *Faithful*

INCARNATION

REDISCOVERING THE SIGNIFICANCE
OF CHRISTMAS

Abingdon Press
Nashville

INCARNATION:
REDISCOVERING THE SIGNIFICANCE OF CHRISTMAS

Copyright © 2020 Adam Hamilton
All rights reserved.

978-1-7910-1641-8

Original hardcover edition is catalogued under
Library of Congress Control Number: 2020941571

20 21 22 23 24 25 26 27 28 29—10 9 8 7 6 5 4 3 2 1
MANUFACTURED IN THE UNITED STATES OF AMERICA

To Sue Thompson
Who incarnated Christ's love
to so many in her role as
my executive assistant
these last twenty-three years.
Congratulations, Sue, on your retirement!

CONTENTS

CONTENTS

INTRODUCTION

Incarnation is both the title and the theme of this book. It comes from a Latin word that means something like "embodiment" or "become flesh." The doctrine of the Incarnation represents one of the foundational, and some might say scandalous, claims of the Christian faith: namely, that the God who created all that is, who sustains the universe by his power, came to us in Jesus. He did not simply inspire Jesus, or speak through Jesus as he might inspire or speak through people today. No, Incarnation claims that God actually became flesh in Jesus.

The church has always struggled with explaining the *how* of the Incarnation, ultimately relying on theological terms like *hypostatic union* and *homoousios* to affirm what our language and understanding find inadequate to explain. I'm content recognizing that the how of the Incarnation will remain a mystery.

My hope in this book is instead to explore the *why* and *to what end* questions of the Incarnation: *Why* would God come to us in Jesus? *What* was the purpose of the Incarnation? *How* are we meant to respond to the Incarnation, to God's coming to us in Jesus, today? In answering these questions, I hope to fulfill the promise of the subtitle of this book—we will rediscover the significance of Christmas, as Christmas is a celebration of the Incarnation.

In each chapter of this book, we'll consider one or more of the names or titles used by the Gospel writers as they introduce the story of Jesus. In Chapter One, we'll focus on the royal titles, Messiah or Christ, and what it means to call Jesus our King. In Chapter Two, we'll turn to the title Savior and in what sense we need saving. In Chapter Three, we'll turn to the name Emmanuel—God with Us—and how in Jesus, God was, and still is, with us. In Chapter Four, we'll turn to the prologue of John's Gospel where we find Jesus called the Word and referred to as light, a passage often read on Christmas Eve. And finally, in the Epilogue, we'll look at what the earliest

Christians meant when they proclaimed that "Jesus is Lord."

The book is intended to be read over five weeks, one chapter a week for each of the four Sundays corresponding to the four Sundays of Advent, with the epilogue read either on Christmas or Epiphany. For those reading the book with others, there are small group videos and a leader guide available. There are also materials available for children and youth—take a look at the back of the book for additional resources.

My prayer as I wrote this book was that God might speak to me, deepening my own faith and understanding, and then that God might speak through me to you. May your faith and understanding grow so that together we might stand in awe of the Incarnation, and in turn incarnate the love of God that came to us in Jesus Christ.

Adam Hamilton
Spring 2020

CHAPTER 1

PRESIDENTS AND KINGS

CHAPTER 1

PRESIDENTS AND KINGS

But you, O Bethlehem of Ephrathah,
who are one of the little clans of Judah,
from you shall come forth for me
one who is to rule in Israel,
whose origin is from of old,
from ancient days.

(Micah 5:2)

In the time of King Herod, after Jesus was born
in Bethlehem of Judea, wise men from the East
came to Jerusalem, asking, "Where is the child
who has been born king of the Jews? For we

15

> *observed his star at its rising, and have come to*
> *pay him homage."*
>
> *(Matthew 2:1-2)*

Every four years, on the first Tuesday after November 1, America elects a president. On that day, we also elect all of the members of the House of Representatives and one-third of the Senate. It's an important day for our nation, but also one that highlights and exacerbates the deep divisions in our society. There will be victory speeches and concession speeches. One person will be the new "leader of the free world."

Two years after the presidential election, the nation votes once more for the entire House and another one-third of the Senate in what is often seen as a referendum on the sitting president as well as the president's policies and party.

In each election, opposing candidates offer competing visions for our nation, conflicting solutions to our problems, and often divergent policies aimed at accomplishing these visions and solving these problems. Combined, they will spend $1 billion or more to get elected. Meanwhile, political action committees will spend another billion, much of it seeking to cast aspersions on candidates they oppose. As much as we decry the polarization, many of us participate in it through our conversations and our use of social media.

Roughly three weeks after Election Day, Advent arrives and Christians prepare to celebrate the birth of their King.

This season puts into perspective all our political wrangling; whatever Christians think about their president, and whoever we voted for in the various elections, we are meant to know that there is only one King. It is to him we give our highest allegiance. While our politics have divided us, Advent should bring us together, uniting us around the newborn King and his life, message, ministry, death, and resurrection.

When I ponder our polarization, and the identity and call of Christ our King, I'm reminded of the words of John Wesley from the preface to his *Explanatory Notes Upon the New Testament*:

> Would to God that all the party names, and unscriptural phrases and forms, which have divided the Christian world, were forgot; and that we might all agree to sit down together, as humble, loving disciples, at the feet of our common Master, to hear his word,

to imbibe his Spirit, and to transcribe
his life in our own![1]

Advent beckons all who consider themselves Christians—regardless of whether they are Republicans, Democrats, Libertarians, or Independents—to come to the stable and there fall on our knees as the shepherds surely did, yielding our allegiance, our hearts, and our will to the newborn King.

In this book, we'll seek to understand who this King is, why he came, and how we might, in Wesley's words, "transcribe his life in our own." In other words, we'll seek to understand the purpose of the Incarnation. We'll do that by considering words and titles used by the prophets, angels, shepherds, and Gospel writers to describe him. As we do, we'll seek to grow deeper in both our understanding of Jesus and our faith in him.

In this chapter, we'll begin by considering the *royal* titles used for Jesus found in the Christmas stories.

Christ/Messiah/King

Matthew begins his telling of the Christmas story with these words: "Now the birth of Jesus the *Messiah* took place in this way" (Matthew 1:18, emphasis added). In Luke's account of the Christmas story, the angel announces Jesus's birth to the shepherds: "Do not be afraid; for see—I am bringing you good news of great joy for all the people: to you is born this day in the city of David a Savior, who is the *Messiah*, the Lord" (Luke 2:10-11, emphasis added).

Messiah is an anglicized version of the Hebrew word *mashiach*. It literally means "anointed" (with oil) or "anointed one," and it refers to an individual or object upon which special oil has been poured as a way of setting the object or person apart for God's purposes. The earliest account in scripture of the use of oil to anoint people or things for God's purposes is in Exodus 28-30. In Exodus 30:22-30, we read:

> *The Lord spoke to Moses: Take the finest spices: ...myrrh...cinnamon...cane...cassia...olive oil; and you shall make of these a sacred anointing oil blended as by the perfumer; it shall be a holy anointing oil. With it you shall anoint the tent of meeting and the ark of the covenant, and the table and all its utensils, and the lampstand and its utensils, and the altar of incense, and the altar of burnt offering with all its utensils, and the basin with its stand; you shall consecrate*

them, so that they may be most holy; whatever touches them will become holy. You shall anoint Aaron and his sons, and consecrate them, in order that they may serve me as priests.

This special oil was made to anoint the furnishings in the Tabernacle used in the worship of God, as well as the anointing of the priests and later the kings. Following this example, Bishop Ruben Saenz took anointing oil and anointed the altar, the baptismal font, and the pulpit at Church of the Resurrection when our congregation completed the central campus's sanctuary. Every time I stand behind the altar to pray over the bread and wine of the Eucharist, or baptize someone at the font, I can still see the oil mark on limestone where our bishop consecrated these items to God's service.

Centuries after the time of Moses, when Israel asked God to give her a human king, God had the prophet Samuel take oil to anoint a man named Saul. First Samuel 10:1 reads, "Samuel took a vial of oil and poured it on his head, and kissed him; he said, 'The Lord has anointed you ruler over his people Israel. You shall reign over the people of the Lord and you will save them from the hand of their enemies all around.'"

From this time on, Israel's kings would be anointed by their prophets and priests. Like the priests and altar furnishings, the anointing of the king happened at God's direction and on God's behalf. It signified that the king was holy to God, set apart for God's purposes, ruling on behalf of God, representing God, and doing God's work.

It's interesting that in many countries, monarchs are still anointed with oil at their coronation. You can see the coronation of Britain's Queen Elizabeth II in video footage taken on June 2, 1953. But the anointing was considered so sacred that it was not allowed to be filmed. A canopy was brought in and held over the queen as the Archbishop of Canterbury poured holy anointing oil from the ampulla (or flask) into the golden coronation spoon. He then dipped his finger into the oil and anointed the queen's forehead, her upper chest, and her hands, consecrating her head, heart, and hands to God. As he did so he whispered, "As Solomon was anointed king by Zadok the priest and Nathan the prophet, so be you anointed, blessed, and consecrated Queen over the Peoples, whom the Lord thy God hath given thee to rule and govern."[2]

Anointing is a sign for the one being baptized, confirmed, or anointed at illness or death that they, too, belong to God, are holy and set apart for God, and that the Holy Spirit's presence is with them.

In the Christian faith, it is not just priests, queens, and kings that are anointed with oil. In many traditions, at baptism, the one being baptized is anointed with oil as a sign that this one belongs to God and is set apart for God's purposes. Many repeat this at confirmation, when the priest or pastor anoints the head of the confirmand with oil, praying for the Holy Spirit to work in and through the one being anointed. Christians also use oil to anoint the sick and the dying. James 5:14 refers to the practice of anointing the sick: "Are any among you sick? They should call for the elders of the church and have them pray over them, anointing them with oil in the name of the Lord." This anointing is a sign for the one being baptized, confirmed, or anointed at illness or death that they, too, belong to God, are holy and set apart for God, and that the Holy Spirit's presence is with them.

On the day I wrote these words, I went to visit my Aunt Carroll, who was dying of liver failure. At the end of our visit, I read scripture and then I opened the anointing oil I keep in a small vial on my keychain. I placed the oil on my thumb, and then slowly and deliberately made the sign of the cross upon my aunt's forehead before praying with her and giving her to God. I told her, "This oil is a sign that you belong to God, that you are God's child, and that sometime soon, he will return for you and welcome you into the kingdom of heaven." Oil is a powerful symbol both in scripture and in the Christian tradition.

Which takes me back to the kings of ancient Israel and Judah. Though prophets, priests, and holy furnishings were anointed, it is the role of king that became most closely associated with anointing in scripture. King Saul, King David, King Solomon, and those who followed after them were hailed as *messiah*—as the Lord's anointed. Among these ancient kings, one became the archetype for all future kings: David.

David: Israel's Archetypal King

David reigned as king from approximately 1010 BC to 970 BC. He was the eighth son of a man named Jesse, a sheepherder in the small town of Bethlehem on the edge of the Judean wilderness. David was also the great-grandson of a woman named Ruth whose story appears in the biblical book that bears her name. God chose the youngest of Jesse's sons when he was just a boy (in his early teens, perhaps even younger). He was a sheepherder, a poet, and musician, and a courageous young man who was described in 1 Samuel 16 as having a complexion that was "ruddy." It was also said that he "had beautiful eyes, and was handsome." Acts 13:22 tells us that God said of David, "I have found David, son of Jesse, to be a man after my heart, who will carry out all my wishes."

David's story is fascinating and looms large in the Bible. He is named over one thousand times in scripture, more often than anyone but Jesus. His story is told across four Old Testament books and a significant number of Psalms were either written by him, commissioned by him, or dedicated to him. He was the archetype (or ideal pattern) for all future kings of Israel. To this day, David is mentioned on street names, hotels, restaurants, and universities across the Holy Land. He was far from perfect, but God loved this man, showed him mercy upon mercy, and used him to shepherd his people.

In regards to David's offspring, God said to David, through Nathan the prophet:

> *I will establish the throne of his kingdom forever. I will be a father to him, and he shall be a son to me. When he commits iniquity, I will punish him with a rod such as mortals use, with blows inflicted by human beings. But I will not take my steadfast love from him, as I took it from Saul, whom I put away from before you. Your house and your kingdom shall be made sure forever before me; your throne shall be established forever.*
>
> *(2 Samuel 7:13b-16)*

This became known as the Davidic Covenant—the promise that a descendant of David would rule over God's people *forever*. That promise had a profound impact upon the Jewish people, who found hope in it during long periods when they were living in exile or when foreign kings ruled over the land. During these times, the prophets recalled

Nathan's promise and affirmed that, despite foreign rulers, the day would come when God would raise up a new king—like David—from David's royal line to rule as a shepherd over God's people.

Ezekiel 34:23-24 provides an example of this hope when the prophet writes, "I will set up over them [Israel] one shepherd, my servant David, and he shall feed them; he shall feed them and be their shepherd. I, the LORD, will be their God, and my servant David shall be prince among them; I, the LORD, have spoken." At this time, the Jews were living in exile in Babylon and David had been dead for four hundred years. Ezekiel wasn't promising that David would return from the dead. He was saying to the exiles that, against all odds, one day a new king, a descendant of David, would rule over God's people once again.

This hope for an ideal king, like David, is what became known as the "messianic hope." The prophets often spoke of this new idealized Davidic king, and even before the Babylonian exile, when David's descendants still reigned in Jerusalem, it shaped their hopes for the ruler. At times, when a crown prince was born, the prophets might offer their visions of what this child would become one day. When a new king was crowned, exuberant hopes for his reign would be uttered by the prophets. There was a longing on the part of the prophets and many of the people for a king from David's royal bloodline who would reign with justice and righteousness. An example of this hope is found in the well-known and much-loved verses of Isaiah 9:6-7:

> *For a child has been born for us,*
> *   a son given to us;*
> *authority rests upon his shoulders;*
> *   and he is named*
> *Wonderful Counselor, Mighty God,*
> *   Everlasting Father, Prince of Peace.*
> *His authority shall grow continually,*
> *   and there shall be endless peace*
> *for the throne of David and his kingdom.*
> *   He will establish and uphold it*
> *with justice and with righteousness*
> *   from this time onward and forevermore.*
> *   The zeal of the LORD of hosts will do this.*

Many interpreters think that Isaiah was using these lofty titles to celebrate the birth of a newborn crown prince around 732 BC, or possibly the coronation of King Hezekiah around 727 BC. This is likely the case, yet with these royal titles, the prophet paints a picture of a king which could never be completely fulfilled by the crown prince or King Hezekiah. Which of these could truly be called Wonderful Counselor, Mighty God, Everlasting Father, Prince of Peace? What earthly king could possibly usher in endless peace forevermore? Hence the words, though given in the context of the birth or coronation of a prince or king in the eighth century before Christ, remained an unfulfilled hope or promise that each successive generation of Jews looked to and built upon, as they imagined and longed for a future king.

Seven hundred years after the time of Isaiah, the Jewish people were yearning for just such a king. Herod the Great ruled over the land, but he was no just and righteous king from David's royal line. And even he ruled only at the pleasure of an even greater king, the emperor in Rome. It was in this context of a deep longing on the part of many for the Messiah to come that the angel Gabriel appeared to young Mary in Nazareth, saying:

"Do not be afraid, Mary, for you have found favor with God. And now, you will conceive in your womb and bear a son, and you will name him Jesus. He will be great, and will be called the Son of the Most High, and the Lord God will give

> *to him the throne of his ancestor David. He will*
> *reign over the house of Jacob forever, and of his*
> *kingdom there will be no end."*
>
> *(Luke 1:30-33)*

There, in the midst of the angel's annunciation to Mary, was the old promise given by God to David through Nathan, that a descendant of David would rule forever. And this child was one of whom Isaiah's royal titles could rightly be used.

Matthew begins his account of Christmas with these words: "Now the birth of Jesus the Messiah took place in this way" (Matthew 1:18). Matthew and Luke want us to know, from the start, that the child whose story they will tell is *the* Anointed One, the long-promised Messiah, the Christ, the Davidic King.

Presidents and Kings

Presidential elections are focal points of power and wealth. The elections of 2020 were anticipated to be the costliest presidential elections to date. At one point, three of the candidates running for president were billionaires, though two eventually bowed out. Early estimates were that over $2 billion would be spent trying to win the race. The winner of such an election will be inaugurated on the western steps of the US Capitol with thousands of people looking on. Following the inauguration, the president will enjoy the inaugural balls with great food, wine, and dancing. He will live in the White House with a crack security team to protect him and his family. He will become not only the "leader of the free world" but the Commander-in-Chief of the most powerful military on the planet.

Contrast that with the King whose birth we celebrate at Christmas. He was born in a stable, with an animal's feeding trough for his bed. He grew up in the obscure village of Nazareth in the first-century Jewish equivalent of "the other side of the tracks." Far from billionaire status, he was trained at making tools and farm implements, doors, and furniture, and likely was skilled as a handyman.*

At the age of thirty, Jesus began his campaign for the office of King. He traveled from town to town, giving various stump speeches about the kingdom of God. In these campaign speeches, he called

---

* The Greek word *tekton* is usually translated as "carpenter," but in an era and place where homes were made of stone or mud brick and built by masons, carpenters worked with wood. They focused on farm implements, doors, shutters, furniture, and whatever else might be made of wood. They could also be what today we'd call a "handyman."

people to love God, their neighbors, and even their enemies. He called his hearers to humility, kindness, integrity, forgiveness, and selflessness. He asked them to care for the hungry, the thirsty, the naked, the sick, the imprisoned, and the immigrant. He decried arrogance and hypocrisy.

His campaign's finance team was a group of people, mostly women, who traveled with his twelve disciples and provided support for his work. The disciples made up the bulk of his campaign staff, but they had never run a campaign before. They were fishermen, a tax collector, and a group of others who had little education—a group some might describe as misfits and ragamuffins—hardly a team most reasonable people would assemble for such an important task.

His campaign trail took him through "all the cities and villages" where he could be found "teaching in their synagogues, proclaiming the good news of the kingdom, and curing every disease and every sickness." As he looked at the people, "he had compassion for them, because they were harassed and helpless, like sheep without a shepherd" (Matthew 9:35-36).

It may seem a stretch to think of Jesus as on a campaign trail, but I think this is how his disciples must have seen his work. They anticipated that at some point in the future he would be installed as king and they would rule with him. Each stop was building support for his reign. He had dinners with leaders. He spoke at huge gatherings with thousands of people. He was constantly talking about his vision, a vision he referred to as the kingdom of God.

Yet, in so many ways, Jesus went about his campaign all wrong—if we're judging by the standards we're used to today. Many of the people wanted a king who would raise an army to push the Romans out of the land—"peace through strength." Jesus instead called his fellow Jews to love the Romans and any other enemies they had. While presidential candidates often court the endorsements of the rich and powerful, Jesus alienated the powerful and influential, and instead associated with the poor and powerless; in the words of Garth Brooks, Jesus had "friends in low places."

Jesus made very few campaign promises—nothing about lower taxes or increased jobs or defeating the Romans. He didn't promise to make Israel a great nation once again. Instead, he spoke about welcoming the stranger, feeding the hungry, clothing the naked, and caring for the sick (see the parables of the good Samaritan and the sheep and the goats for examples of his campaign platform). His kingdom would entail self-denial and taking up one's cross. He urged his followers to let their lights shine by their good deeds and in this way, people would be drawn into the Kingdom. In his kingdom, he promised that the grieving would be comforted, those who hungered for righteousness would be filled, the merciful would be shown mercy, and the meek would inherit the earth.

Jesus urged his followers to let their lights shine by their good deeds and in this way, people would be drawn into the Kingdom.

The citizens of this Kingdom would seek to do God's will. They would love God with all their hearts, souls, minds, and strength, and they would love their neighbors as they love themselves. The ethics of this Kingdom would involve each citizen treating others as they wish to be treated and demonstrating selfless love. Can such a Kingdom really exist on earth? Jesus asked his disciples to pray to God for this: "Your kingdom come. Your will be done, on earth as it is in heaven" (Matthew 6:10). Everything he taught them was about living as citizens of this Kingdom. Yet he recognized while on trial with the Roman governor just before his death, "My kingdom is not from this world" (John 18:36). It wasn't, but he seemed to think it could be present as his followers yielded their hearts and lives to God. Which is why he once said to his disciples, "The kingdom of God is among you" (Luke 17:21) or as in the King James Version, "The kingdom of God is within you."

Jesus's Anointing and Coronation

We've learned that *messiah* means "anointed one," but in its most common usage, it was another way of saying "king." Just as Jesus's campaign was not what we'd expect from one seeking to rule, his anointing and coronation were likewise out of the ordinary. Typically, the king was anointed with oil by the high priest, or a prophet like Samuel, just as Britain's queens and kings are anointed by the Archbishop of Canterbury. But Jesus's anointing came not at the hands of the high priest, but at the hands of three women.

One of these women, in Luke 7:36-48, was described as a "sinner," likely a prostitute, to whom

Jesus had shown love and mercy. She didn't dare anoint his head with oil, but only his feet, and she did this while he was eating at the home of Simon the Pharisee. A second woman anointed his head shortly before his arrest, while he was eating at the home of Simon the Leper (Matthew 26:6 and Mark 14:3). In John's Gospel, Mary, the sister of Martha and Lazarus, anoints Jesus's feet while he eats at their home, also just days before his arrest (John 12). In all three of the instances (some scholars believe they are the same story remembered differently by the Gospel writers), a woman seeking to honor Jesus anoints him, unaware that this act points to his role as the Messiah, the anointed one, the King.

Jesus's coronation happens at the hands of Roman soldiers, the same men Jesus called his followers to love. They plaited a crown of thorns and pressed it upon his brow, wounding his sacred head. His exaltation occurred as they stripped him, nailed him to a cross, and hoisted it into the air. There he hung slowly dying for hours, a king nobly laying down his life for his people. The sign above his head stating his crime read, "The King of the Jews" (Mark 15:26).

This, of course, was not the end of the story for our King. After his burial Friday afternoon, he lay in the tomb through the next day, the Sabbath. But on Sunday morning, the stone covering the mouth of his tomb was tossed aside as our King conquered death. He appeared first to the women who followed him, then to the disciples, and ultimately to hundreds of others. He called them to continue the work that he had begun, teaching what he'd taught and initiating others into his kingdom through baptism, so that together they might live as his people, praying and working for God's kingdom to come. God's reign is expanded with each person that chooses to follow Christ as their King, living the gospel he proclaimed.

The Return and Final Triumph of the King

While he was with them, Jesus spoke to his disciples about a final judgment, when the "Son of Man" or "Human One"—a phrase he uses frequently in Matthew, Mark, and Luke to refer to himself—would return. Various New Testament epistles anticipate a day when history as we know it will be brought to a close, and when, in the words of Revelation 11:15 (set to music in Handel's *Messiah*), "The kingdom of this world / Is become the kingdom of our Lord, / And of His Christ, and of His Christ; / and He shall reign for ever and ever." On that day, evil will be utterly defeated. The writer of Revelation offers this compelling vision of Christ at the end of time as we know it:

> *Then I saw heaven opened, and there was a white horse! Its rider is called Faithful and True, and in righteousness he judges and makes war. His eyes are like a flame of fire, and on his head are many diadems.... On his robe and on his thigh he has a name inscribed, "King of kings and Lord of lords."*
>
> *(Revelation 19:11-12a, 16)*

A few verses later the author of Revelation, in his vision of an eternal kingdom, hears a voice shouting:

> *"See, the home of God is among mortals.*
> *He will dwell with them;*
> *they will be his peoples,*
> *and God himself will be with them;*
> *he will wipe every tear from their eyes.*
> *Death will be no more;*
> *mourning and crying and pain will be no more,*
> *for the first things have passed away."*
>
> *And the one who was seated on the throne said,*
> *"See, I am making all things new."*
>
> *(Revelation 21:3-5)*

We live in that period between the triumph of Easter and Christ's triumphant return when he makes all things new. We see a world where suffering still occurs, where darkness seems to reign, where the kingdoms of this world seem to have the upper hand. We continue to live as followers of the King whose kingdom is not of this world, but breaking into this world through his followers—through us.

This is what Jesus spoke of when he compared the kingdom of God to leaven that leavens the whole batch of dough. It is what he meant when he told his disciples that they are like salt that preserves and flavors all it touches. Or when he described the Kingdom as a mustard seed that starts small but grows into a bush that the birds of the air take refuge in.

> *Jesus is the single most influential person to have walked this planet.*

Today, nearly a third of the world's population claims Jesus as their King. Far more have been influenced by the things he taught, the values he espoused, the life he lived. I don't believe it is an overstatement to say that he is the single most influential person to have walked this planet. For those who count him as King, as I do, we awaken each day recognizing that our highest allegiance, our deepest devotion, and our greatest commitment is not to country or political party or even to family, but to Jesus the Christ, our King, whose kingdom is the climax of human history. Each morning, as any who've read my books knows, I fall to my knees and once more pledge my life to him: Here I am Lord, send me.

And though we live in that time between triumphs, the triumph of the Resurrection and that of the Second Coming, the first gives us confidence in the second. The resurrection of Jesus leads us to be, in the words of Zechariah, "prisoners of hope." One of the great preachers of the twentieth century, James Stewart, in his book, *King Forever*, notes:

> The world's dark night may still continue pressing in upon us, but if I have seen Christ, then I know that the darkness of history is now shot through with unquenchable hope and with the final certainty of the glorious outcome

39

of all its struggles. Or to make it more
personal I may go down into the dark,
but if I do, I am still in the hands of
him who bears the scepter of all the
universes and everlastingly makes all
things new, here and hereafter, and
therefore I am safe forever.[3]

If you have any Jewish friends with whom
you have prayed, you have likely heard the words,
"Barukh ata Adonai Eloheinu, Melekh haolam"
recited during prayer. They translate, "Blessed are
you, Lord our God, King of the Universe." Christians
who hold a Trinitarian understanding of God believe
that this King chose to walk among us. The Father
sent the Son that the world might know who this
King of the universe really is, and that they might
hear his call, know his will, and live as his people.
The Son, in turn, sent the Spirit to empower us to
incarnate the love of Christ.

As I write these words, an old friend has just
died. Her name was Nancy Brown, and she was a
force for the kingdom of God. She woke up every
day seeking to serve Jesus as her King. She'd known
abuse as a girl, but rather than destroying her, it
made her strong, compassionate, and determined to

bring good from her pain. Nancy had served in the state legislature, believing that politics was a calling from God, a ministry in which she could work to develop just laws and compassionate policies that would positively affect not only her constituents, but the entire state.

Nancy had been to Africa several times before she finally twisted my arm hard enough that I agreed to go with her. She took me to a rural community in Zambia where she was greeted by singing children and single mothers welcoming "Mama Nancy" back again. She had raised money and brought together leaders to build fishponds, other agricultural projects, a feeding program, a health clinic, and a school for these children. I'd never seen anything like it. But this was only the first of many projects Mama Nancy supported. Her vision and tireless spirit were driven by the belief that we were not only to pray, "your Kingdom come, your will be done," but also to work to make this a reality.

I don't know your politics, but if you are a Christian, I know your King. His Sermon on the Mount, his parables, and his great commandments calling us to love God and neighbor represent the laws of his kingdom. Our allegiance to him comes above all other allegiances. As we conclude this chapter, I'd like to invite you to join me in yielding your life to Christ and pledging to follow him as your King.

Blessed are you, our God, King of the universe. You came to us in Jesus to show us who you are and who you call us to be. I yield my life to him. Jesus, be my Christ, my Messiah, my King. To you, O Lord, I offer my time, my talents, my resources, my influence, and my all to you. Help me live in such a way that I honor you in all that I do. Amen.

CHAPTER 2

THE SAVIOR AND OUR NEED FOR SAVING

CHAPTER 2

THE SAVIOR AND OUR NEED FOR SAVING

[An] angel of the Lord appeared to him in a dream and said, "Joseph, son of David, do not be afraid to take Mary as your wife, for the child conceived in her is from the Holy Spirit. She will bear a son, and you are to name him Jesus, for he will save his people from their sins."

(Matthew 1:20b-21, emphasis added)

In that region there were shepherds living in the fields, keeping watch over their flock by night.

Then an angel of the Lord stood before them, and the glory of the Lord shone around them, and they were terrified. But the angel said to them, "Do not be afraid; for see—I am bringing you good news of great joy for all the people: to you is born this day in the city of David a Savior, *who is the Messiah, the Lord. This will be a sign for you: you will find a child wrapped in bands of cloth and lying in a manger."*

(Luke 2:8-12, emphasis added)

Excited about Christmas, a little boy was finishing a letter to Santa with a list of the Christmas presents he badly wanted. And then, just to make sure he had covered all of his bases, he decided to send his Christmas wish list to Jesus as well. The letter to Jesus began, "Dear Jesus, I just want you to know that I've been good for six months now." Then it occurred to him that Jesus knew this wasn't true.

After a moment's reflection, he crossed out "six months" and wrote "three months." He thought some more, then crossed out "months" and replaced it with "weeks." "I've been good for three weeks," his letter now read. Realizing Jesus knew better than this, he put down his paper, went over to the Nativity set sitting on a table in his home, and picked up the figure of Mary. He then took out a clean piece of paper and began to write another letter: "Dear Jesus, if you ever want to see your mother again…"*

If we're honest, I suspect none of us could write a letter to Jesus claiming that we had been perfectly good for six months, or even three whole weeks. There's a little naughtiness in us all.

Shortly after learning from Gabriel that she was to become pregnant by the power of the Holy Spirit, and that she would give birth to the Messiah, Mary shared this news with Joseph. Joseph became the first person in history to doubt the story Mary told; he would not be the last.

That night, Joseph undoubtedly tossed and turned in his bed, probably feeling hurt, angry, and disappointed at what he believed was Mary's infidelity. But after finally falling asleep, he had a dream. In that dream, an angel of the Lord appeared to him saying, "Joseph, son of David, do not be afraid to take Mary as your wife, for the child conceived in her is from the Holy Spirit. She will bear a son, and you are to name him Jesus, *for he will save his people from their sins*" (Matthew 1:20-21, emphasis added).

---

* Variations of this joke have been passed around by preachers for decades.

In Luke 1:31, the angel Gabriel tells Mary, too, that her child's name should be *Jesus*.

Jesus is an anglicized version of the Greek version of his name. But the Hebrew is *Yeshua*, a shortened version of *Yehoshua*. It comes from the personal name for God in Hebrew, *Yahweh*, and the word for "to save" or "to deliver," *yasha*. *Yeshua* therefore means "God saves," "God delivers," or "God helps." Jesus's name points to his role and the purpose of the Incarnation. He came as God's instrument of deliverance or salvation. Every time we speak his name, we recognize him as our Savior, Deliverer, Rescuer, and Helper.

Despite the fact that the New Testament represents only about a quarter of the entire Bible, Jesus's name appears more than any other person in scripture, over 1,600 times. With each mention of his name, we are reminded that he is our Savior and Deliverer.

The angel speaking to the shepherds on that first Christmas night announced to them, "I bring you good tidings of great joy, which shall be to all people. For unto you is born this day in the city of David a *Saviour*, which is Christ the Lord" (Luke 2:10-11 KJV, emphasis added).

Yet what does it mean to call Jesus a Savior? Why do we need a Savior? What do we need saving from? How does he save us? These are questions we should ask as we journey through the season of Advent. Let's consider a few possible responses.

"Are You Saved?"

Perhaps you've heard Christians speak of being "saved." Maybe you've been asked, "Are you saved?" Some Christians point to a day and time when they were saved. Other Christians, no less saved, may use different words to describe the day they put their trust in Jesus, or their experience of Christ's deliverance and grace and its impact on their lives.

I came to faith at fourteen with the help of a terrific pastor, youth pastor, and my friends in a small Pentecostal church I had begun attending. I was "saved" one night about 11:00 p.m. after I finished reading the Gospel of Luke. I got down on my knees, asked Jesus to forgive my sins, and offered my life to him. From that day on, I've sought to follow him.

If you asked me then what I meant when I said I was saved, I think my fourteen-year-old self would have said that in accepting Christ as my Savior, I received forgiveness for my sin and I was saved from

49

the guilt that was the result of my sin, and from the punishment my sins deserved—hell. Today, I'd say that the salvation Jesus offers is far more expansive than simply forgiveness and deliverance from hell.

I tend not to use the term "saved" because it seems like insider language to some, and the meaning of salvation and being saved seems unclear at times, even to those who use the term. Nevertheless, it is a biblical term, used about 150 times in the New Testament, and one that Christians of all types use in hymns.

Here's where I find it helpful to remember that the Hebrew word *yasha* and the Greek word *sozo*—both of which can be translated in their various forms as *saves* or *saved*—can also be translated as *deliver(ed)*, *rescue(d)*, or *help(ed)*. When we speak of Jesus as Savior, and of his work of saving us, we are speaking of his work to deliver, rescue, or help us.

As you study how the word *save(d)* is used in the New Testament, you'll find it has a variety of meanings. The word is sometimes used to describe physical healing, forgiveness, rescuing from one's enemies, rescuing from disasters, deliverance from suffering, an internal transformation upon placing one's faith in Christ, and God's deliverance at the last day. Adding to the confusion, the term is used in various tenses. Jesus and the New Testament authors at times speak of *having been saved*—a past action reflecting what Christ has done to save and our acceptance of that salvation. Paul speaks of our *being saved*—a continuing action of salvation occurring in the present but not yet completed. And we also find both Jesus and the apostles using the future tense describing those who *will be saved* ("those who endure to the end will be saved" is an example).

There are many ways in which Jesus saves us and many things he saves us from. Let's consider just a few.

Saved from Sin

Let's begin with the words of the angel to Joseph, "He will save his people from their sins."

As I think about these words, I'm reminded of someone who once said to me, "Why do Christians spend so much time talking about sin?" For some people, it feels like sin is the only thing they hear about in church. I want to be clear: if all you ever hear about in church on Sunday is sin, you're probably in the wrong church. But if you never hear about sin in church, you may also be at the wrong church. The good news of Jesus is not that we're sinners, but that he is our Savior. But we can't appreciate his role as Savior if we don't know we need to be saved!

> ## *The good news of Jesus is not that we're sinners, but that he is our Savior.*

As we think about being saved from our sins, it might be helpful to first define sin. In both the Old and the New Testaments, the words most commonly translated as *sin*—in Hebrew, *hata*, and in Greek, *hamartia*—mean to stray from the path or to miss the mark. This implies that there is a right path, a mark, or an ideal that we're meant to follow as human beings—a path, target, or mark we routinely struggle to remain upon or to hit. By our nature we are, in the words of the great old hymn "Come, Thou Font of Every Blessing," "prone to wander, Lord, I feel it, prone to leave the God I love." In the New Testament, sin is used to describe both the inner predisposition or inclination to stray from God's path (our nature) and the actual act of straying (our actions).

The path we're meant to live, the ideal we were created to pursue, is laid out throughout scripture. It includes practicing justice, demonstrating loving kindness, and walking humbly with God (Micah 6:8). It includes sharing your food with the hungry, clothing the naked, and having compassion for the sick, the stranger, and the prisoner (Matthew 25:35-45; Isaiah 58:6-10). It is captured in the Ten Commandments, Jesus's Sermon on the Mount and his parables, the words of the prophets and the apostles, and much more. Jesus summarized the path with two commandments Moses had been given: Love God with your entire being, and love your neighbor as you love yourself. The latter he summarized again with the Golden Rule: "In everything do to others as you would have them do to you" (Matthew 7:12). Do you always walk this path? I fail too many times to count.

If everyone walked this path, we would have no wars, we would need no prisons, and we wouldn't see refugee crises or have a world where people die of malnutrition. There would be no more racism or bigotry. All marriages would survive. There would be no sexual assault, no cruelty, no dishonesty or unkindness anymore. But that is not the world we live in. Why don't we have that kind of world? The Christian answer is sin.

As humans we all struggle with sin. Christianity asserts that sin is the fundamental problem in the human condition. Again, when the Bible speaks of sin, it means both the innate *tendency to stray* from the right path and also the *act of straying*. It is both the interior struggle with temptation—the war within us between right and wrong—and the act of succumbing to temptation when we stray from the path. The result is suffering, alienation, guilt, and shame.

This conflict is captured right from the start in scripture with the archetypal story of Adam and Eve in the garden of Eden. Eden represents the world as it was meant to be, with no suffering or pain. Adam and Eve were given one rule: Don't eat from the tree of the knowledge of good and evil. All other trees were theirs to eat from, just not this one. The talking serpent in the garden beckoned them to eat the fruit, promising them that if they ate it they would become like God. They saw the fruit was beautiful and they surmised it must be delicious, and they ate. And with that, paradise was lost.

The story is not intended to teach us ancient history. It is meant to teach us about ourselves. We know there is a good and right path ("you may freely eat from any other tree, but don't eat the forbidden fruit"), but we have all heard the whisper of the tempter encouraging us to turn from that path. We've all known the battle with temptation, the tendency to do the wrong thing, and we've all heard the serpent whisper to us, rationalizing with us, beckoning us to leave the path.

On many occasions, I've sat with people as they confessed their sins—affairs, addictions, stealing, gambling, lying, and a thousand other sins that leave the individual feeling guilty and ashamed, and often painful consequences. For many of us, our sins may not seem so obvious. Pride may be the most dangerous of sins from which all others flow and can destroy us from the inside out.

What is the forbidden fruit the serpent beckons you to eat? The lie he tells you to lead you astray or to trip you up? Where do you stray from the path or miss the mark?

When I was a young adult, the most obvious of the sins I wrestled with was lust. Gluttony eventually joined lust and then overshadowed it. Later, it was indifference (what others call *sloth*); my failure to act in the face of injustice or to address the suffering of others. The twin sins of greed and envy eventually had a go at my heart, leading me to squander what I had on things that could not satisfy. I've known what it was to get angry over things that didn't matter; impatient and short-fused, I've said things I later regretted. But often underlying all of these has been pride. You may recognize that list I've just recounted; they are known as the "seven deadly sins." Most of us wrestle with these sins and with their children.

Eating too many cookies after supper or the bit of envy you felt when you saw your neighbor's new car, dog, lawn mower, or big screen television is not the end of the world. However, you should carefully examine the source of the genuine suffering in the world, and you'll find one or more of the deadly sins just beneath the surface.

Paul captured this battle in Romans 7:18-19 when he wrote, "I can will what is right, but I cannot do it. For I do not do the good that I want, but the evil I do not want is what I do." He later continues:

> *So I find it to be a law that when I want to do what is good, evil lies close at hand....But I see*

in my members another law at war with the law of my mind, making me captive to the law of sin that dwells in my members. Wretched man that I am! Who will rescue me from this body of death? Thanks be to God through Jesus Christ our Lord!

(Romans 7:21-25)

Paul referred to his body as a "body of death" because of the desires that lurk within. Who is it that delivers him or saves him? "Thanks be to God through Jesus Christ our Lord!" Jesus is our Savior, Deliverer, Helper, and Healer.

Wrestling with the Devil

Jesus saves us both from our inner tendency to sin, and the guilt and shame we carry with us when we do sin. When we choose to follow Christ, we find a new center to our lives and a change in our inner desire. It is not that temptation completely vanishes from our lives, but we find a new, stronger impulse pulling us toward the right path. We find our hearts transformed, little by little. As our inner nature is being changed, our thoughts, words, and deeds change, and we find ourselves more often and intentionally walking the good path.

The more we seek to grow in him, follow him, love him, and serve him, the more we recognize the tempter and his fast-talking ways.

The more we seek to grow in him, follow him, love him, and serve him, the more we recognize the tempter and his fast-talking ways.

Paul spoke of our struggle with sin in terms of a battle or a wrestling match. He wrote, "Finally, be strong in the Lord and in the strength of his power. Put on the whole armor of God, so that you may be able to stand against the wiles of the devil" (Ephesians 6:10-11). James 4:7 tells us, "Resist the devil, and he will flee from you." Some Christians see the devil as a metaphor or personification of temptation and evil—in some ways, a name for the innate tendency in every person to disobey God. It is the inner and outer pull toward leaving God's good path. For many other Christians, the devil is a literal spiritual being who plays the role of tester, tempter, and accuser in scripture.

However you perceive the devil, faith in Jesus gives us strength to resist the tempter. Asking for

Christ's help gives us power to "stand against the wiles of the devil."

My experience, after forty-two years of being a Christian and attempting to walk with Christ daily, is that I am still tempted to think, say, or do things God does not intend. But when I turn to Christ, I sense his strength, his help, and his deliverance. He has transformed, and is transforming, my inner desires. We call this *sanctification*—the process by which the Holy Spirit changes our hearts and minds so that we become the people God intended us to be.

Martin Luther captured this ongoing battle well in "A Mighty Fortress Is Our God," his famous hymn:

> A mighty fortress is our God,
> a bulwark never failing;
> our helper he amid the flood
> of mortal ills prevailing.
> For still our ancient foe
> doth seek to work us woe;
> his craft and power are great,
> and armed with cruel hate,
> on earth is not his equal.
>
> Did we in our own strength confide,
> our striving would be losing,
> were not the right man on our side,

the man of God's own choosing.
Dost ask who that may be?
Christ Jesus, it is he;
Lord Sabaoth, his name,
from age to age the same,
and he must win the battle.

When the angel announced that Mary's child would "save his people from their sins," we usually read that as pertaining to forgiveness. It certainly includes that. But even more important is Christ's transforming work in our lives, drawing us to God's path, strengthening us and delivering us from our inner compulsion to sin. When Jesus speaks of being born again, and Paul speaks about being a "new creation" in Christ, they are speaking of this work of transformation, this saving us from our sins.

I can say this with confidence: I'm not the person I hope to be yet nor am I the person Christ wants me to be, but I'm also not the person I would have been were it not for his rescuing grace in my life. I am a better husband, father, and human being because of Christ. I am more generous, compassionate, and kind than I would have been without his influence in my life. I'm less of a jerk than I would have been had he not begun rescuing me. He has saved me from my sin and he *is saving* me from my sin. And that is true of all who call upon him as Savior.

Much of the goodness, kindness, and compassion in the world today happens as a result of the way that Christ has saved his people from their sins. This ongoing work of deliverance or salvation is what we ask when we pray the Lord's Prayer: "deliver us from evil," or in some modern translations, "rescue us from the evil one" (Matthew 6:13). It is in his witness, his love, his impact upon our soul, and his Spirit's work that he is saving us from our tendency to sin.

Forgiveness of Sins

In addition to the inner battle in which Jesus becomes our hope and help—saving us from the tendency to sin—he also saves us from the ill effects of our sin. I don't mean that he removes the natural consequences of our sins. If we do something that hurts someone else, we have to work to heal this pain, to make amends. If you do something illegal, you may go to jail. Jesus doesn't save us from these consequences. What he saves us from is the guilt, shame, and sense of alienation from God that we feel when we sin. He forgives our sins, washing us clean and making us new.

A conversation I recently had with a young woman illustrates the power and importance of this. She recounted something she'd done recently that had left her feeling embarrassed, ashamed, and very far from God. Have you ever felt this way? I have.

I reminded this woman of the many stories in the Gospels of people who, like her, had done things that left them feeling shame, guilt, or embarrassment. Together, we considered the story in Luke 7 concerning the woman who wept at Jesus's feet, a woman Luke describes simply as "a woman in the city, a sinner." She sensed Jesus's compassion and love, barged into the home of a Pharisee where Jesus was a dinner guest, and there she fell at Jesus's feet, pouring precious ointment on his feet as she wept. Jesus forgave her sins and said, "Your faith has saved you" (Luke 7:50). We considered what this story and the many other Gospel stories of forgiveness tell us about the people Jesus loved and his compassion and mercy for them. Then we prayed, asking Jesus to show this same compassion and mercy to her.

The New Testament has a host of words to describe this work: Christ *redeems* us, *restores* us, *reconciles* us, *justifies* us, and *forgives* us, to name just a few. How does he do this? Some see his redemptive work mechanistically, transactionally, or juridically: Jesus, God in the flesh, the one holy and righteous man who ever lived, died in our place for our sins. It is noted that his death was a full and sufficient payment for our sin. Sometimes this makes perfect sense to me. When we have sinned, we feel guilt, shame, and a need to atone. We see Christ offering himself, suffering for us, and praying from the cross, "Father, forgive them; for they do not know what they are doing" (Luke 23:34). Christ died for us in our place. You've likely heard it said, "We owed a debt we could not pay. Christ paid a debt he did not owe." This is one way of understanding his atoning work.

Others see Jesus's death on the cross, and the various ways the New Testament speaks of his death, through the lens of John's prologue where John speaks of Jesus as "the Word"—God's incarnate effort to speak to humanity. Christ's death is seen less in transactional terms and more in terms of God's attempt to speak to us about sin, mercy, and love.

Jesus's death is seen not as a payment required in order for God to forgive, but a dramatic act in which God conveys our need for forgiveness, the costliness of grace, and the depth of God's love and mercy. It is not about *procuring* God's forgiveness, but *proving* God's love and forgiveness. Paul notes in Romans 5:8, "But God proves his love for us in that while we still were sinners Christ died for us." In the Crucifixion scene in the Gospels, Jesus holds a mirror up to humanity. This act demonstrates the height of human sin and brokenness; when the Incarnate God walked among us, humans crucified him. But the cross is also a magnifying glass allowing us to see the pain God experiences as a result of human sin. In Genesis 6, God sees the violence of humanity and is grieved to his heart by it. On the cross, the Incarnate God is tortured to death—a dramatic picture of how our sin affects God. And on the cross, in Jesus's death, in his offering himself for us, in his prayer, "Father, forgive them," he demonstrates the lengths to which God is willing to go—the price God is willing to pay—to rescue us from ourselves and from our sin. Such an offering must be full and sufficient for our sins. We must know there is nothing more that must be done for our forgiveness than the Incarnate God offering himself for us. Finally, as we will consider further below, Jesus's death on the cross is meant to convey to us not only the depth of God's love, but also to paint a picture of the selfless love Christ calls his followers to demonstrate.

Jesus's death on the cross is meant to convey to us not only the depth of God's love, but also paint a picture of the selfless love Christ calls his followers to demonstrate.

Seen this way, the cross is a divine drama, a sermon fleshed, God's Word to humanity—a Word that has the power to lead us to repentance, to an awareness of the costliness of God's grace, to accept that our sins are truly forgiven, and to see the depth of God's love. Christ does give himself to atone for our sin, not as a kind of juridical transaction, but as an act of selfless love, offering himself on our behalf that we might be saved by his selfless love.

I believe this is what Dietrich Bonhoeffer was getting at when he wrote some of his most compelling words about the cost of discipleship:

> Grace is *costly* because it calls us to follow, and it is *grace* because it calls us to follow *Jesus Christ*. It is costly because it costs a man his life, and it is grace because it gives a man the only true life. It is costly because it condemns sin, and grace because it justifies the sinner. Above all, it is *costly* because it cost God the life of his Son: "ye were bought at a price," and what has cost God much cannot be cheap for us. Above all it is *grace* because God did not reckon his Son too dear a price to pay for our life, but delivered him up for us. Costly grace is the Incarnation of God.[4]

We cannot save ourselves, but God, in his great love for us, comes to us in Jesus to save us from our sin and its consequences, and to restore us, redeem us, and heal us. I need that salvation and so do you. He can save you from yourself, from your brokenness and tendency to sin, making you the person God created you to be. And he can save you from the times you've stumbled, from guilt and shame.

There's far more that can and should be said about this, but this is a start. Let's turn to the other ways in which Jesus saves us.

Saved from Hopelessness, Meaninglessness, and Despair

Everyone experiences an existential crisis at some point in their lives, likely more than once. These crises are moments when we question the meaning of our existence. We wonder if our life has any value or worth. We may feel like there is no reason to go on living.

I sat across the table from a man recently who told me that he had planned his exit strategy. He had been contemplating taking his life; he no longer believed his life had any meaning or purpose. I listened to what he was feeling. Knowing he had a deep faith that spanned decades, I asked him, "Do you believe God sees your life as worthless right now?" He wasn't sure. I shared with him, "Jesus's life, his words, his ministry, his death and resurrection all shout that your life has value and worth. Jesus spent most of his time with people I suspect felt much as you do. Some had known tremendous loss. Others experienced terrible failures. Some had been humiliated and others felt alone. But to each—to the prostitute, the demoniac, the woman who'd been married and divorced five times, the leper and all the rest—Jesus's words and ministry said the same thing: 'You matter to God. Your life has meaning. God isn't done with you yet.' As Jesus suffers and dies on the cross, he is saying to you and me and the rest of humanity, 'Your life has value. Your sins are forgiven. You are loved.' And in his resurrection Christ shouted, 'I know you feel hopeless, but look, I have overcome and you will too.'"

Our conversation ended with my sharing suicide prevention resources and offering support from the congregation's care team, gaining his promise of reaching out and his assurance he would not hurt himself. Then we prayed. I mention this not to share the details of what was discussed, but to remind you that the Incarnation was about, in part, Christ walking with us, speaking to us, and demonstrating for us the love of God and our value and worth. It was about saving us from despair.

Jesus was continually ministering with the people that religious folk of his day considered uncouth, less important than others, and unclean. The Hebrew term for them was *am ha'aretz*—at the time, it was a derogatory term that meant "people of the land." While Jesus associated with wealthy and deeply devoted religious people, too, his real interest was in the non-religious and nominally religious of his time—people who were marginalized by the religious leaders. These included the chronically sick, the mentally ill, the people considered outsiders by those who made up the religious establishment. His message to them was consistent: you matter to God.

He conveyed this by the way he healed the sick. He communicated it in the parables of Lazarus and the rich man, the prodigal son, and the sinner and the tax collector. He demonstrated it in his care for the woman caught in the act of adultery, his offer of living water to the woman at the well, his words of affirmation to Zacchaeus the tax collector, and his call of Matthew the tax collector. He showed it in his close relationship with Mary Magdalene out of whom he cast seven demons, his healing of the demon-possessed man who lived among the tombs, his calling of the fishermen to be his disciples, and many more acts of outreach and welcome to those who needed him.

What Jesus said to all of these people was that their lives had meaning, that they were valued by God, that God *wanted* them. To borrow the words of existentialist theologian Paul Tillich, they were "accepted by God." This is the essence of grace. Based upon nothing that they (or we) had done, they were accepted by God. And because they were accepted, their lives (and ours) find meaning. Their lives were purposeful. They were to follow Jesus, to love God, and to love other people. They were to bear much fruit, and to care for the hungry, the naked, the immigrant, and the sick. They were to let their "light shine before others." They were to be the "salt of the earth." They were to "seek first the kingdom of God." They were to serve one another.

Here is what I said to the man who told me he had wanted to exit this world: When God is finished with you, he'll take you. But until then, he has work for you to do. Even in your pain, your feelings of failure, your sense of hopelessness, Jesus is with you. He continues to walk with you and he plans to use you. Jesus had nothing, not even a place to lay his head, yet he knew he had work to do. You are loved by God. Jesus came to tell you that. You are forgiven by him. He came to show you that. You are valued by God. He died to prove this to you. I cannot promise you that your troubles will be cleared up, or that you won't have future problems if you just pray hard enough. In fact, Jesus promised that in this world, we would have troubles. But this is what I can say: Jesus is not finished with you yet; he will walk with you and he will work in and through you. Your task is to trust him and to keep following him.

In Jesus, God came to us to save us from the despair that comes from believing there is no meaning to life or to our lives in particular. He came to save us from our sense that we have no value and worth, and that there is no reason to go on. He came to rescue us from feeling there is no hope. With him by our side, there is always hope.

Having spent thirty years walking with my congregation through the challenges of their lives, I've learned this: there is always hope. When we trust in Jesus and we seek to do the next right thing, somehow things will work out. Paul noted this from a prison cell in his short epistle to the Philippians. He believed that even in his imprisonment, God was at work. If he was released, he would go on serving God. If he died, he would be with Christ, which he saw as far better than remaining on this earth. Life may not work out as we hoped, expected, or prayed. But placed in God's hands, things work out. We survive the downturn in the economy and eventually crawl out of the financial hole we're in, or file bankruptcy and start again. We find that our lives are actually more joyful in our small apartment and our simpler lifestyle than they were when we lived in our mini-mansion.

> *Life may not work out as we hoped, expected, or prayed. But placed in God's hands, things work out.*

I recently spoke with a woman who was preparing to get remarried. I remembered when her husband left her years ago: the tears, the pain, the sense of abandonment. But here she sat with the man she had been dating for the last year, and she said to me, "I never knew it could be like this. I never knew someone could love me so much." She began crying, only this time, they were tears of joy.

Even those who faced the unimaginable—the loss of a child or a spouse—survived. They healed. They would never lose the scars or the bitterness of the loss, but they did survive and found, as Paul described, that "suffering produces endurance, endurance produces character, and character produces hope" (Romans 5:3-4). Their deep sorrow shaped in them character and compassion, and defined their lives in the most beautiful of ways. I saw this recently in a couple whose daughter died a year ago. They were at the home of another couple in our congregation whose son had just died, planting flowers in the backyard of the newly grieving family. The couple was a living witness that you can survive even the most terrible of losses. Jesus's life, his death, and his resurrection save us from hopelessness and despair.

You Are Loved

In 1967, Barnett Helzberg of Helzberg's Jewelers—a national jewelry store that's headquartered in Kansas City—developed a marketing campaign built around the theme, "I am loved." His girlfriend Shirley had just accepted his proposal for marriage and he knew that he was loved; from this came the idea of giving people small, clip-on buttons that said, "I am loved." The initial order of 50,000 buttons was gone in a heartbeat, and millions more were ordered. More than fifty years later, you can still find these buttons at Helzberg's as well as jewelry that bears this slogan.

Everyone longs to be loved. It is a fundamental need we have as human beings: to believe that you are valued by someone and treasured by someone else, that you matter to them.

Barnett Helzberg recognized that, for most people, the aim of giving jewelry was to say to the recipient, "I love you," and for that person to feel as they wore the jewelry, "I am loved." The jewelry was a sign that came at some cost and communicated to the recipient how much they are loved.

This is one way of seeing the life, death, and resurrection of Jesus. He came as an expression of the love of God. Christina Rossetti captures this truth so beautifully in her 1885 poem, "Love Came Down at Christmas" (now a beloved Christmas carol):

> Love came down at Christmas,
> Love all lovely, Love divine;
> Love was born at Christmas;
> star and angels gave the sign.
>
> Worship we the Godhead,
> Love incarnate, Love divine;
> worship we our Jesus,

but wherewith for sacred sign?

> Love shall be our token;
> love be yours and love be mine;
> love to God and all men,
> love for plea and gift and sign.

Rossetti was one of the foremost poets of her time, a woman who had known her own existential crises and bouts of depression. She suffered from Graves' disease and later breast cancer. But it was in her faith in Jesus that she found hope, help, and peace. Among her other hymns is "In the Bleak Midwinter," also a Christmas carol, which ends with these words:

> What can I give him,
> poor as I am?
> If I were a shepherd
> I would bring a lamb;
> if I were a Wise Man,
> I would do my part;
> yet what I can I give him:
> give my heart.

Love came down at Christmas to a stable in Bethlehem, to two poor parents and a handful of night-shift shepherds. That love would be evident in the way he healed the sick, forgave sinners, welcomed children, fed the hungry, and cared for his disciples. But nowhere was that love more clearly seen than on the cross as he hung there, saying, "This much. God loves you this much."

That is what John was saying in one of the Bible's best-known verses, John 3:16: "For God so loved the world that he gave his only Son...." It was what Jesus was communicating when he said to his disciples, "No one has greater love than this, to lay down one's life for one's friends" (John 15:13). When we look at the cross, we see what Methodist pastor Alexander Means wrote in his beloved hymn of the early 1800s: "What wondrous love is this, O my soul, O my soul, what wondrous love is this, O my soul! What wondrous love is this that caused the Lord of bliss to bear the dreadful curse for my soul, for my soul, to bear the dreadful curse for my soul."

When my daughters were growing up, I tried to convey to them how much I loved them. I could think of no greater way to convey my love than to say, "I love you so much, I would give my life for you and I wouldn't have to think about it. That's how much I love you."

That is precisely what Jesus does for us in his life and his death. He saves us from *lovelessness*. You are loved regardless of what anyone else might say. You are loved regardless of how unloved you may feel at this particular moment. You are loved.

You are loved regardless of what anyone else might say. You are loved regardless of how unloved you may feel at this particular moment. You are loved.

It was that sense of his love that had the greatest impact on me when, as a teen, I trusted in him for the first time. It was a time when my mother and I had been fighting. We had just moved to a new home in a new school district and I had very few friends. My folks were divorced. I remember lying on my bed feeling utterly friendless, alone, and unloved. In that moment I heard a voice, not audibly, but as a thought that permeated my brain. It seemed to come from outside of me, speaking into me. I felt Jesus speaking to me. The voice said, "Adam, it doesn't matter if no one else wants you or loves you. *I* wanted you and *I* love you, and that's all that matters." At that moment I felt as if Someone were holding me. I felt such a powerful sense of peace.

When I speak with people who feel utterly unloved, it is this idea that most impacts them. We all long to be loved. Christ came to Incarnate God's love. I love how Paul notes, in these beautiful verses, "For I am convinced that neither death, nor life, nor angels, nor rulers, nor things present, nor things to come, nor powers, nor height, nor depth, nor anything else in all creation, will be able to separate us from the love of God in Christ Jesus our Lord" (Romans 8:38-39). This love that came down at Christmas—a love that was most radically seen on the cross—is a love that will not let us go.

Saved from Death

Finally, the greatest existential crisis we face as human beings is death. It is an enemy we cannot cheat or avoid. But in his death and resurrection, Jesus not only triumphed over evil, hate, and sin, but he defeated death itself. Paul captured well the powerful impact of Christ's resurrection when he noted, "Death has been swallowed up in victory"

(1 Corinthians 15:54b).* Jesus once said, "I am the resurrection and the life. Those who believe in me, even though they die, will live…" (John 11:25). When we trust this, we find it changes how we face the grief and anxiety of death.

Over the years, I have spent a lot of time with people who are dying and with their close family members. The resurrection of Christ does not take away all the pain and loss of death, but it does offer a powerful antidote to death and its accompanying grief. Christ's resurrection makes it clear that death does not have the final word. It changes our perspective on our loss.

Sharon's husband, Irv, had been getting weaker and weaker as he lay in the care center. She was not allowed to visit him due to concerns about COVID-19. So her visits involved standing outside the building, often accompanied by their children, visiting through the window. As he approached the end, he would blow kisses to her from the bed. They'd been married 65 years and friends since they were in second grade. Several days later they took Irv to the hospital. Since she could not go in with

---

* In these words, Paul is drawing from Hosea 13:14 with a nod to Isaiah 25:8, both from the Greek translation of the Old Testament.

him, she sat in her car in the the parking lot, as close as she could be to him. It was there, as we spoke by phone, that she told me, "I will miss him terribly." She began to cry, then continued, "But I also know that Irv belongs to Christ, and I have no doubt that he will be safe with Jesus." The next day he died and as we spoke following his death, we prayed and gave her lifelong companion to Jesus, remembering Jesus's words, "I am the resurrection and the life. Those who believe in me will never die."

Jesus, the Incarnate God, makes it clear that he "holds the keys of Death and of Hades" (Revelation 1:18), and that "because I live, you also will live" (John 14:19). Jesus saves us from death.

The angel told Joseph in a dream to give Mary's child the name *Jesus*: God Saves. The angels brought good news of great joy to the shepherds, telling them that day, in the city of David, was born a Savior. Jesus saves us from sin, guilt, and shame. He rescues us from loveless, meaninglessness, and hopeless lives. And in the end, he delivers us from death. This is why we call him Savior.

Jesus, I need you to save, rescue, deliver, and heal me. I trust in you as my Savior. Save me from my sin and from myself. Save me for you and your purposes. Save me by your love and for your love. Save me from despair and give me hope. Help me to trust in your resurrection, that I might face death not with fear, but with hope. Amen.

CHAPTER 3

EMMANUEL IN THE MIDST OF A PANDEMIC

CHAPTER 3

EMMANUEL IN THE MIDST OF A PANDEMIC

"Joseph, son of David, do not be afraid to take Mary as your wife, for the child conceived in her is from the Holy Spirit. She will bear a son, and you are to name him Jesus, for he will save his people from their sins." All this took place to fulfill what had been spoken by the Lord through the prophet:

Incarnation

"Look, the virgin shall conceive and bear a son,

> *and they shall name him Emmanuel,"*

which means, "God is with us."

> *(Matthew 1:20b-23)*

Long ago God spoke to our ancestors in many and various ways by the prophets, but in these last days he has spoken to us by a Son, whom he appointed heir of all things, through whom he also created the worlds. He is the reflection of God's glory and the exact imprint of God's very being, and he sustains all things by his powerful word.

> *(Hebrews 1:1-3)*

For several weeks, people in the US had been hearing about a new, highly contagious virus and the respiratory illness it produced in those who contracted it. First reported in Wuhan, China, around Christmastime in 2019, the virus killed thousands there and the Chinese government took radical steps to keep it from spreading. Yet, Wuhan seemed far away from everyday life in America.

But during the second week of March 2020, everything changed in America. That week all but one state in the union confirmed cases of the coronavirus. The outbreak was still relatively small—about three thousand confirmed cases with sixty deaths. But the virus was spreading exponentially. The death rate of one to two percent of those who fell ill from the virus was considerably higher than the mortality rate from a typical flu.

That week, the nation took unprecedented steps to address the invisible threat. The NBA suspended its season. The NCAA canceled March Madness. In New York, Broadway theatres went silent. The nation's art galleries closed. Disney's theme parks shut down. Universities across the country suspended classes, then local school districts everywhere announced students would not be coming back to their classrooms until the fall. Mayors, then governors, then the President of the United States declared a state of emergency. Churches closed their doors and those who could opted to broadcast worship via the internet. Senior living centers and nursing homes were placed on lockdown, not allowing visitors in to see residents. Essential functions and services were maintained, but most everything else shut down. America had closed.

All of this uncertainty, fear, and concern over the impact to the economy spread to the markets. The stock market began seeing huge gyrations, losing 35 percent of its value before starting to recover. Within weeks, twenty-six million people were out of work.

Some spoke of the concern and mass closings as hype and hysteria, an overreaction to a "flu bug." Meanwhile, the Centers for Disease Control and Prevention (CDC) looked at a worst-case scenario in which 1.7 million Americans, mostly over sixty, might die as a result of COVID-19, the name of the disease caused by the new coronavirus. No one anticipated this would be the case, but there was grave concern that hospitals might overflow with patients, resulting in a lack of ventilators to help those with severe cases of the disease to survive.

Fear and panic are in the air as I write these words. Our pastors and staff have been working each day to be a calming presence, to engage our church members in serving others, and to help them know that God is with us in the midst of this battle. As of this day, 140,000 people have died of COVID-19, including eight of my parishioners or their family members. By the time you read this, many more people will have died from the disease.

In biblical times, there were pandemics—the Bible calls them "pestilence" or "plagues." Pestilence is mentioned more than fifty times in the Bible. The biblical writers and their contemporaries did not know about germs that cause diseases. They could not see the microscopic genetic machines we call viruses that hijack healthy cells and use them to replicate their unhealthy genetic codes. When faced with an outbreak of disease, their only conclusion was that the rapid spread of illness which killed thousands of people must have been the work of God.

Understandably, some are saying similar things today—that the pandemic must be the will of God. Some believe God sent the coronavirus pandemic to punish us, to teach us, or to bring good out of us. I don't believe that.

Today, we have a basic understanding of viruses: what they are, how they mutate and spread, and how they attack our bodies. We devote resources to develop anti-viral treatments and vaccines. If we believed these viruses were sent by God, then aren't researchers and doctors who strive to prevent and combat them fighting against God? But that's not what we believe. Instead, we fight against these viruses because we believe that the indiscriminate deaths of grandparents, parents, and even children is *not* God's will.

I do not believe that God sent the coronavirus, but I do believe he is with us in the midst of this pandemic, doing what God always does—comforting, leading, consoling, and wringing good from the adversity and pain. There will be plenty of silver linings from this frightening turn of events. Even now, in the midst of the pandemic, the world has changed in so many ways for the better. There is tragedy and death, but there is life, hope, goodness, and love.

> ### *There is tragedy and death, but there is life, hope, goodness, and love.*

Books are written and submitted for publication months before they go to press. You hold this book in your hand knowing how the battle against the coronavirus played out. You know if the school and business closures and quarantines helped to "flatten the curve" and slow the spread of the virus, thus saving lives. I'm writing in the midst of the storm, knowing things may get worse before they get better. I sit here bracing for what lies ahead, but I do so with hope—a hope that is rooted in Advent and Christmas.

What does the pandemic have to do with Advent and Christmas? Everything, I think.

Fear is in the air today, as it was again and again in the lives of God's people in the Bible. Over one hundred times in scripture, God, an angel, a prophet, the psalmist, or Jesus himself said to someone, "Don't be afraid." Why not fear? Consistently the answer was because "God is with us." This response is at the heart of the Christmas story; it is the essence of the Incarnation. The God who has always been with his people came to us, in the flesh, in Jesus.

As Matthew wrote the opening to his Gospel, retelling the Christmas story and reflecting on the significance of the birth of Jesus, he offered these words: "All this took place to fulfill what had been spoken by the Lord through the prophet: 'Look, the virgin shall conceive and bear a son, and they shall name him Emmanuel,' which means 'God is with us'" (Matthew 1:22-23).

This was a remarkable connection Matthew made with the words of Isaiah, and an essential insight about the meaning of Christmas and the significance of Jesus. No other New Testament author cited these words of Isaiah. In this chapter, we'll explore Isaiah's words concerning this name, *Emmanuel*, why Matthew used it to refer to Jesus, and what it means for us to call Jesus *Emmanuel* today.

Isaiah's Prophecy

Let's begin by turning the clock back approximately 735 years before the birth of Jesus. At this time in Israel's history, the kingdom that David and his son Solomon had ruled two centuries earlier had split into two kingdoms. If you think of the American Civil War between the North and the South, that's a little like what happened to the kingdom of Israel after the death of Solomon. Nine of the original twelve tribes of Israel broke away and formed what became known as the Northern Kingdom.* These nine tribes retained the name

---

* We often refer to the north as being made up of "ten tribes" of Israel, but this is not entirely accurate. The Northern Kingdom was made up of the tribes of (1) Ephraim, (2) Dan, (3) Reuben, (4) Gad, (5) Issachar, (6) Zebulun, (7) Naphtali, (8) Asher, and (9) Manasseh. Manasseh received two major portions of the land of Canaan, each designated for a "half-tribe" of Manasseh. Levi, whose tribe was assigned no property, included descendants living in both the north and the south. Judah included, as noted above, Judah, Benjamin, and Simeon.

Israel for their kingdom, but they rejected Solomon's son, Rehoboam, as their king. To make matters a bit more confusing, the prophets sometimes referred to the Northern Kingdom as Ephraim after the tribe whose land included the capital of the north, Samaria. And even more confusing, at times they referred to the Northern Kingdom simply as Samaria, after its capital city.

To the south, the Southern Kingdom came to be known as Judah after the largest and most dominant tribe in this region. This kingdom was made up of the tribes of Judah, Benjamin, and Simeon. Its capital was Jerusalem and its people remained loyal to Solomon's son, David's grandson, Rehoboam, after the northern tribes broke away. Levites served the religious needs of the community in both the Northern and Southern Kingdoms. A map of the two kingdoms and their constituent tribes can be found on page 94.

By Isaiah's time, the two kingdoms had been divided for almost two hundred years. Despite their differences, the Northern and Southern Kingdoms still shared history, language, religion, and culture. Sometimes, they were military allies who joined against a common enemy. At other times, they fought each other.

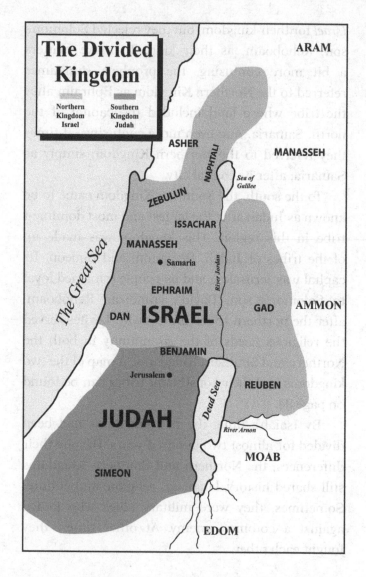

The Divided Kingdom

Northern Kingdom Israel
Southern Kingdom Judah

ARAM

ASHER

NAPHTALI

MANASSEH

Sea of Galilee

ZEBULUN

ISSACHAR

MANASSEH

The Great Sea

• Samaria

River Jordan

EPHRAIM

DAN   ISRAEL

GAD   AMMON

BENJAMIN

Jerusalem •

Dead Sea

REUBEN

JUDAH

River Arnon

MOAB

SIMEON

EDOM

That takes us to the context of the Immanuel prophecy in Isaiah.* Around 735 BC, the Northern Kingdom of Israel formed an alliance with the kingdom of Aram—located in what is today western Syria. Israel and Aram hoped to rebel against the dominant superpower of the day, the Assyrian Empire, freeing themselves from Assyrian control and the payment of heavy taxes to the Assyrians. To do this, they needed Judah's help and support. But King Ahaz of Jerusalem refused to join their coalition.

As a result, the kings of Aram and Israel prepared to attack Judah, planning to kill Ahaz and to install a king favorable to their plans, one who would lead Judah's armies into battle with them against the Assyrians. This was terrifying to Ahaz and to the people of Judah. Isaiah 7:2b notes, "...the heart of Ahaz and the heart of his people shook as the trees of the forest shake before the wind." It was then that God told Isaiah the prophet to find King Ahaz and to say, "Take heed, be quiet, do not fear, and

---

* *Immanuel* is spelled with an I in Isaiah and *Emmanuel* with an E in Matthew. That is because of a difference in how the word is spelled in Hebrew and Greek. In this chapter, I'll use Emmanuel when speaking of the passage in Matthew and Immanuel when referring to Isaiah.

do not let your heart by faint because of these two smoldering stumps of firebrands" (Isaiah 7:4). The two smoldering stumps referred to the kings of Israel and Aram. Then God promised that the harm the two kings sought to do to Ahaz would not happen, provided Ahaz would stand firm in his faith.

That takes us to the sign of Immanuel. God essentially said to Ahaz, "Ask me for a sign that what I've promised will happen, that these two kings will be no threat to you." But Ahaz refused to ask for a sign. In response Isaiah tells Ahaz:

> *"Therefore the Lord himself will give you a sign. Look, the young woman is with child and shall bear a son, and shall name him* Immanuel. *He shall eat curds and honey by the time he knows how to refuse the evil and choose the good. For before the child knows how to refuse the evil and choose the good, the land before whose two kings you are in dread will be deserted."*
> *(Isaiah 7:14-16, emphasis added)*

The events that led to this word from Isaiah occurred around 735 or 734 BC. Isaiah's prophecy unfolded just as he foretold. A young woman—the Hebrew word for young woman, *almah*, can mean a young woman, an unmarried young woman, a virgin—"is pregnant" (*harah* in Hebrew, which usually signifies one is already pregnant) and will give birth to a son. In its original context, this is referring to a young woman of Ahaz's time, perhaps a young woman the king has married or a new wife of Isaiah. This young woman has become pregnant, will give birth, and she will name her son *Immanuel*. This child will be a visible sign of God's promise to put an end to the threat of these two kings Ahaz fears. God tells Ahaz, before the boy is old enough to know right from wrong—perhaps pointing to the child at age three or four, or maybe when he becomes a man at twelve or thirteen—the two kings and their kingdoms will be abandoned.

In 732 BC, when the child was two or three, the Assyrians attacked both Aram and Israel, and forcibly relocated some of their people to Assyria. This may have been the fulfillment of the prophecy. But it seems more likely the prophecy refers to Immanuel at age twelve or thirteen. In the year 722 BC, the Assyrian army marched on the Northern Kingdom of Israel and destroyed it, taking the rest of her people into exile. And in 720 BC, Aram was destroyed as well, precisely as God had foretold through the prophet.

The child, Immanuel, whose name meant, "God is with us," was a living sign of God's promise to Ahaz both that God was with him, and that God would protect Ahaz and the people of Judah.

Isaiah was one of the most important books of the Hebrew Bible for Jesus, as it was for the early church. The New Testament contains more than sixty allusions or direct quotations from Isaiah. Many of them point to a particular way of reading the book. Much of what Isaiah prophesied was, as we've seen above, addressing the specific circumstances of the prophet's day or the near future. It foretold how God was about to work at that time the book was written. But every generation of Jews that followed Isaiah's time looked at his words in light of their own time, and heard in them a picture of how God might work in their time as well. Early Christians also read Isaiah this way, typologically, seeing in Isaiah's words a type or pattern that was being repeated in their own time or, for Christians, how God had worked in and through the life of Jesus.

That is how Matthew read Isaiah 7:14 and the promise of a child whose name would be called Immanuel. Let's turn now to Matthew's Gospel.

The Incarnation

This is how Matthew tells the Christmas story:

Now the birth of Jesus the Messiah took place in this way. When his mother Mary had been engaged to Joseph, but before they lived together, she was found to be with child from the Holy Spirit. Her husband Joseph, being a righteous man and unwilling to expose her to public disgrace, planned to dismiss her quietly. But just when he had resolved to do this, an angel of the Lord appeared to him in a dream and said, "Joseph, son of David, do not be afraid to take Mary as your wife, for the child conceived in her is from the Holy Spirit. She will bear a son, and you are to name him Jesus, for he will save his people from their sins." All this took place to fulfill what had been spoken by the Lord through the prophet:

> *"Look, the virgin shall conceive and bear a son,*
> *and they shall name him Emmanuel,"*

which means, "God is with us." When Joseph awoke from sleep, he did as the angel of the Lord commanded him; he took her as his wife, but had no marital relations with her until she had borne a son; and he named him Jesus.

(Matthew 1:18-25)

Notice the birth is just five words: *she had borne a son*. The rest of the story is largely about the Annunciation to Joseph as he slept, making it clear that the child Mary was carrying was conceived by the Holy Spirit. Matthew emphasizes this twice in these verses. And then, to address the implications of this unique conception, Matthew draws upon Isaiah 7:14: "All this took place to fulfill what had been spoken by the Lord through the prophet: 'Look, the virgin shall conceive and bear a son, and they shall name him Emmanuel,' which means, 'God is with us.'"

As we've seen, the child whose birth Isaiah had foretold with these words was an ordinary child who lived in the eighth century before Christ, to serve as a sign of God's presence with King Ahaz. But for Matthew, that first Immanuel was a foreshadowing of Jesus. There is no evidence that Mary ever called Jesus *Emmanuel*. The name is not mentioned anywhere else in the New Testament. Matthew alone found in this somewhat obscure verse a powerful picture of who Jesus is and why he came.

The emphasis on Jesus's conception by the Holy Spirit seems to be Matthew's way of pointing to his unique identity. By virtue of this unique conception, this child to be born would somehow be both Son of Man and Son of God. The idea that Jesus was the Son of God is a major theme in Matthew. Seventeen times in Matthew, Jesus is identified as the "Son of God" or "God's Son." Twice in the Gospel, God speaks from heaven (at Jesus's baptism and on the mount of Transfiguration) saying, "This is my Son, the Beloved, with whom I am well pleased." In the temptations in the wilderness, the devil tempts Jesus to question his identity as the Son of God, or to prove it. When Jesus encounters the demons, they can't help but acknowledge that he is God's Son. Jesus regularly refers to God as his Father and doesn't deny any claims when others call him the Son of God.

Matthew does not offer us a fully developed Trinitarian theology of how God is at once Father, Son, and Holy Spirit. He offers us no clear explanation for how Jesus could be fully God and fully human, as the Council at Nicaea would attempt to do three hundred years after Jesus's birth. But throughout the Gospel, Jesus is shown to do the things we would expect God to do. He heals the sick, opens the eyes of the blind, forgives sinners, miraculously feeds the multitudes, and even raises the dead. He controls nature, walks on water, casts out demons, and conquers death. In a way that was never true for Isaiah's Immanuel, God was with us in this Emmanuel, Jesus.

This is what we mean when we speak of the Incarnation: God took on flesh and entered our world as a human being.

Incarnation: God Experiences Humanity

This is what we mean when we speak of the Incarnation: God took on flesh and entered our world as a human being. It is clear in scripture that Jesus is not merely God wrapped in human flesh—God in a body. He *became human* in Jesus. He experienced what we experience as humans. In Jesus, God experienced temptation, love, hunger, joy, fear, friendship, grief, doubt, rejection, a sense of abandonment by God, and death. He wept, he bled, he suffered, he died. There is something profoundly moving about God actually knowing what we are experiencing *as humans*.

We have a team of amazing nonpaid staff members at Church of the Resurrection called Congregational Care Ministers (CCM). They are gifted, called, and trained to care for our members as they walk through adversity. Most have experienced some pain themselves. Some have lost children; some lost family members to suicide. Some have been through divorce, job loss, or cancer. When a member of Resurrection loses a child, they are grateful that I, or one of our other passtors, stopped by to care for them. But there is a qualitative difference in care when a CCM who has lost a child themselves comes to care for these grieving parents. It makes a difference when their caregiver has actually walked in their shoes, knows their pain, and has survived the darkness they are walking through. This makes all the difference.

This is in part what is so powerful about the idea of the Incarnation. God doesn't just imagine what it's like to be human—how could an all-powerful God *really* know what it is like to be weak, scared, tempted, or hurt—in Jesus, he *became* flesh. The apostle Paul quotes what was likely an early hymn of the church in Philippians 2, using the word *ekenosen* ("emptied") to describe the Incarnation. In

Jesus, God "emptied himself" of his divine power to experience life as one of us.

God knows the smell of rain on a summer day. He's tasted a meal of warm bread and smoked fish with a glass of wine. He knows the joy of sharing it with good friends. He's seen, with the same eyes we see with, the beauty of a sunset. He's known how the human heart feels when it loves deeply and the intensity of grief when a good friend dies. He knows what it feels to laugh and cry, to be angry and afraid—not as the omniscient, all-powerful, omnipresent God—but as we experience these things: in the flesh.

He also experienced the same frailties, frustrations, temptations, and desires of the flesh we experience. As a boy, he chafed under his parents' authority just as many of us did (see Luke 2:41-52). As a teen, he knew raging hormones. As a young man, he surely felt the burning desire of lust. He knew anger, impatience, pride, and the ease with which we can say and do things that hurt others. He knew the temptation to drink too much. He knew the lure of wealth and power. Hebrews 4:15 notes that Jesus was "tested as we are, yet without sin."

When you come to God, pouring out your heart, asking for his help, or praying for his forgiveness, you pray to one who *knows*—who understands what it is to be fallible, frail, and fearful. This is the power of the Incarnation.

From the moment it was released in 1995, I loved Joan Osborne's hit, "One of Us." The song repeatedly asks listeners, "What if God was one of us?" Osborne then asks what we might think if God came walking on this planet, "just a slob like one of us." To me it's a Christmas carol, capturing the essence of the Christian gospel.

The notion that God might show up looking human is not so hard to believe. Plenty of Hollywood films have done a great job developing this idea. I think of *Evan Almighty* and *Bruce Almighty*. Perhaps my favorite movie in this vein was *Oh God!*, which was released in 1977. In that movie, the recording artist John Denver played an assistant manager in a grocery store who considered himself an atheist. God is played by George Burns, a short, elderly man who wore thick glasses and a ball cap. In the film, God revealed himself to a skeptical John Denver, began to prove to him that he really was God, and called him to become an apostle.

In the movie, God *appears* in human form. God could have chosen to be a man or woman of any color or shape. The Creator who spoke the world into being certainly would have the power to do that. But that is not what Christianity professes to have happened. It teaches that God in Jesus did not simply assume human appearance but, in some mysterious way, actually was born and lived as a human being.

Incarnation: God Reveals Himself to Humanity

I recently had a conversation with a young man in my congregation who was struggling with his faith. I had baptized him as an infant and been his pastor his entire life. He was at college and a friend of his, an atheist, was raising good questions that he'd struggled to answer. Among these was, "If there really is a God, why doesn't he just show himself to us?" He asked me, "Pastor Adam, have you ever seen God?"

I began by reminding him that the universe is, by some calculations, about ninety-three billion light-years across (a light-year is how far light travels in a year at approximately 186,000 miles per second).

Some suggest the universe is far larger still. God created all of it, stands outside and beyond it, while at the same time God's presence permeates it all. God animates the cosmos, sustains it, and holds it together.

God animates the cosmos, sustains it, and holds it together.

Moses once said to God, "Show me your glory." God replied, in essence, "You could not survive the experience." A couple of years ago, we had a terrific solar eclipse in Kansas City. Everyone was gearing up to see it. But do you remember the warnings given at a solar eclipse? Again and again we were told, "Don't look directly at the sun during the eclipse. You could seriously damage your eyes." We bought special glasses to be able to see. This concern for our eyesight was over looking at our relatively modest star, the sun, even as it was being obscured by the moon. The universe is thought to contain between two hundred billion and two *trillion* galaxies, each containing billions of stars like our sun. They reflect God's glory, which is greater than the total of these combined! Like Moses we say, "Show us your glory." And God says, "Really?"

The psalmist recognized this: "The heavens are telling the glory of God" (Psalm 19:1). Yes, I have seen God, or at least a reflection of him, in the world around us. The sun, moon, and stars, the beauty of the earth from the highest mountains to the marvel of human DNA—it all reveals God.

But I told this young man, the God whose glory fills the cosmos actually did what you asked, and what Moses asked, and what every thoughtful human being has asked—he did come to show himself to us in a way we could see. He came to us in Jesus. He is, the scripture says, "the image of the invisible God" (Colossians 1:15). The author of Hebrews writes, "He is the reflection of God's glory and the exact imprint of God's very being" (Hebrews 1:3a). Jesus said to his disciples, "The Father and I are one" (John 10:30), and "Whoever has seen me has seen the Father" (John 14:9).

So, yes, I see God through the world that God has made, I told this young man, but I see God most clearly when I look at Jesus.

When I picture what God is like—God's character, love, mercy, and grace—I see Jesus. I see him loving broken people, eating with sinners and tax collectors. I see him healing the sick and restoring vision to those who were blind. I see him touching the lepers who were treated as untouchables and restoring them to the community by healing their affliction. I see him coming upon a funeral procession and sharing the grief of a mother who had lost her son, and then raising the young man back to life. I think about the Jesus who cast out demons from those who were mentally ill or plagued by forces greater than themselves. I think of the compassion he showed to the prostitute who wept at his feet. I think about the Jesus who said, "the Son of Man came to seek out and to save the lost" (Luke 19:10). When I pray, I pray to the God who showed me what God is like, thanks to all the ways that Jesus revealed God's heart. This is what Emmanuel means to me.

Incarnation: God Is with Us

Matthew begins his Gospel telling us that Jesus is "God with us"—Emmanuel. At the end of his Gospel, he recounts Jesus's final words to his disciples, "I am with you always, to the end of the age" (Matthew 28:20). It is not just that God *was* with us in Jesus, but that Jesus *continues* to be with us. He is still Emmanuel. And because I believe he is with me, I live differently; I have peace, I find strength, I live seeking to walk with him.

When I visit someone in the hospital, I take the person's hand and sometime before I leave I say, "I came here to be a physical reminder that Jesus is with you. Feel my hand. I came to remind you that Jesus is with you here in this room, all the time."

Because God is with us, we need not fear.

Because God is with us, we need not fear. Throughout the Bible, the Israelites would become afraid, as King Ahaz was in Isaiah's day. God's response was always the same. It is captured in Deuteronomy 31:6: "Be strong and bold; have no fear or dread of them, because it is the LORD your God who goes with you; he will not fail you or forsake you." The Incarnation was God's way of putting flesh on this promise; God is with us.

For many years, our family dog was a beagle named Maggie. Maggie was a surprise Christmas gift to my wife and children when the girls were ten and thirteen. I loved this little dog. She grew up with my daughters; even after they became adults and left home, she was still there to greet me at the door when I'd get home every day, tail wagging and eager for my companionship. As she grew older and her vision faded and she couldn't hear, she'd always be at my feet. I think she felt safe when I was around.

On a summer day in 2014, Maggie and I were home alone as I worked on my sermon for the weekend. I noticed that she was acting strangely. Thinking she needed to go outside, I took her out into the yard. She stumbled and fell down, and then lay in the grass. She appeared to be having a stroke. She was panting and appeared frightened. I was certain she was about to die. I lay down next to her in the grass, stroked her head with one hand, and wrapped my other arm around her as I repeated to her over and over, "Maggie, it's okay, it's okay. I'm right here."

Maggie survived that brush with death and lived for another couple of years before finally succumbing to death at the age of sixteen. When she died, my wife LaVon and I were both with her, holding her and telling her once more, "Don't be afraid, Maggie; we're here with you." I've been with a lot of people who died, including grandparents I truly loved, but I've never cried as hard as I did that day when

Maggie died. She'd been my daily companion for sixteen years.

When I think of the Incarnation, I think of these two experiences with Maggie. In Jesus, God came to us to be with us in our fear, our struggles, and our pain. Matthew was right to call him, *Emmanuel*, "God with us."

Our Mission—to Incarnate the Love of God

That leads me to one concluding thought. Jesus came to incarnate God's presence and love to humanity. But before he left this earth, he called us to do the same in his name. Jesus's followers are intended to put flesh on the invisible God, to incarnate God for the world. We know what this looks like because we see incarnation in Jesus as we read the Gospels. Paul notes that the church is "the body of Christ." We are the ongoing incarnation.

Dr. Philip Ireland was an emergency medicine physician in Liberia during the terrible Ebola outbreak a few years ago. When the epidemic started, some Western doctors fled the country. But Dr. Ireland wasn't leaving, these were his people

Then he came down with the deadly virus. During the night he thought might be his last, he was in a hospital ward, lying on a plastic sheet. He vomited and had diarrhea so many times, he finally passed out. The next morning, he awoke, as he recounts, "barely alive, in a sea of mess."

That is when a physician's assistant named Patrick came to him, cleaned him from head to toe, dressed him in clean clothes, placed him in a bed, prayed for him, and encouraged him. Dr. Ireland wrote, after he recovered, "His act of love towards me, to wash me, was so much so that I will never forget it in my entire life." This physician's assistant was Emmanuel for Dr. Ireland. He incarnated—he put flesh on—the presence, love, and mercy of God.[5]

Most of us will never be called upon to care for Ebola patients, though by the time you are reading this, there will be many stories of those who cared for persons with COVID-19. But all of us are called to follow Emmanuel, and in turn, to incarnate his presence and love to others.

Jesus is God with us. Because he is Emmanuel, Jesus knows and understands you, including your temptations, struggles, pain, and afflictions. Because he's Emmanuel, he is able to show you who God is and what God is like. As Emmanuel, he seeks to remind you that he is *always* with you and you don't need to be afraid. He calls you to go in his name to incarnate God's love to others.

O come, O come, Emmanuel.

Oh God, how grateful we are that you came to us in Jesus Christ, our Emmanuel. You understand our humanity, our fears, our weaknesses, our succumbing to sin, those moments when we are less than what you wish us to be. You understand our love, our hurts, and our pain. You understand our struggle with grief and death. Thank you for revealing yourself to us in Jesus, that we might know who you are and that we might walk with you and love you all of our days. Lord, use me to be Emmanuel for those who don't know you. Help me to incarnate your love and grace to all that I meet. In Jesus's name. Amen.

CHAPTER 4

THE LIGHT OF THE WORLD

CHAPTER 4

THE LIGHT
OF THE WORLD

*In the beginning was the Word, and the Word
was with God, and the Word was God. He was
in the beginning with God. All things came into
being through him, and without him not one
thing came into being. What has come into being
in him was life, and the life was the light of all
people. The light shines in the darkness, and the
darkness did not overcome it.*

(John 1:1-5)

Again Jesus spoke to them, saying, "I am the light of the world. Whoever follows me will never walk in darkness but will have the light of life."

(John 8:12)

[Then Jesus said to his disciples,] "You are the light of the world. A city built on a hill cannot be hid. No one after lighting a lamp puts it under the bushel basket, but on the lampstand, and it gives light to all in the house. In the same way, let your light shine before others, so that they may see your good works and give glory to your Father in heaven."

(Matthew 5:14-16)

A pastor friend of mine wrote to tell me of two little boys who were spending the night at their grandmother's the week before Christmas. The grandmother saw them off to bed and then retired to her bedroom, leaving the boys to say their customary bedtime prayers. The younger boy spoke first and shouted his prayer in a loud voice: "Dear God, I want a bicycle for Christmas! Amen!" His older brother said, "Why are you yelling? God's not deaf." "No," the younger boy replied, "but I think Grandma is!"

While most of us grew up knowing that Christmas is meant to be the celebration of the birth of

Jesus, the real action was sitting around the tree opening the presents. As exciting as it is to open gifts, whether they are bicycles or Barbie dolls or whatever else we've hinted that we want, I've noticed something over the years. Regardless of your age, if you have thoughtfully created or purchased a gift for someone else—a gift that is meaningful to you—there is more joy in watching others open your gift than in you opening the gifts of another. I noticed this last year as my five-year-old granddaughter stopped opening her presents to see me open what she had made for me; she became animated telling me all about it. I saw this in my daughters and my son-in-law in the gifts they gave. And I felt this from my wife, particularly with the photo book she had created for me of a trip we'd taken. I feel it myself, when watching the kids open gifts I've picked out for them. As Jesus said, it really is more blessed to give than to receive, particularly when we've spent time preparing or choosing a thoughtful gift.

But what if you've carefully chosen, maybe even created, a gift for someone else, and they opened it and quickly set it aside with little more than a quick thank you? Or worse, perhaps there was not a word at all. It's a most unsatisfying feeling and perhaps even a bit hurtful.

I write books in part for me, to deepen my own faith and understanding. And I write them for you, the reader, praying that somehow these books touch you, teach you, encourage you, and inspire you. I wrote this little book hoping to help us to see the true gift of Christmas—to ponder and reflect upon it, to understand the mystery and meaning of the Incarnation. Thus far, we've considered the titles used of Jesus found in Matthew's and Luke's accounts of the Christmas story: *Messiah*, *Savior*, and *Emmanuel*. Mark doesn't record the Christmas story, but begins with John the Baptist's preaching and Jesus's baptism as a man of about thirty years of age. Even so, Mark introduces Jesus as the Messiah/Christ, the Savior (using his name, *Jesus*), and God's Son. In this chapter, we turn to John's telling of the Christmas story and the titles he uses to describe Jesus.

Second-century church father Clement of Alexandria noted the difference between John's Gospel and the Synoptic* Gospels (Matthew, Mark, and

---

* "Synoptic" is derived from Greek and means "to see together." It is used of Matthew, Mark, and Luke because, despite their differences, they tell the story of Jesus in much the same way.

Luke), describing John as the last of the Gospels written. He called it the "spiritual Gospel." We see that from the start in John's account of Christmas. Absent are the stories of Mary and Joseph. There's no journey to Bethlehem, no shepherds, no wise men, no birth in a stable—but my, how rich is John's account of Christmas.

At the Church of the Resurrection every year, we postpone John's telling of the Christmas story until the climax of the candlelight Christmas Eve service. We dim all the lights in the sanctuary. Then we extinguish the altar candles and the four Advent candles we lit during the four weeks of Advent. As we do, we remind the congregation that we cannot appreciate the light that Christ brings until we linger in the darkness for a moment. With each candle we extinguish, we name the darkness: pandemics, wars, famines, economic hardship, hopelessness, despair, hurt and pain, grief and death. We sit there in the darkness for a moment. Babies crying, children antsy, we sit there craving the light. Then we read these words as one small candle enters the room:

In the beginning was the Word, and the Word was with God, and the Word was God. He was in the beginning with God. All things came into being through him, and without him not one thing came into being. What has come into being in him was life, and the life was the light of all people. The light shines in the darkness, and the darkness did not overcome it.

. . .

He was in the world, and the world came into being through him; yet the world did not know him. He came to what was his own, and his own people did not accept him. But to all who received him, who believed in his name, he gave power to become children of God, who were born, not of blood or of the will of the flesh or of the will of man, but of God. And the Word became flesh and lived among us, and we have seen his glory, the glory as of a father's only son, full of grace and truth.

(John 1:1-5, 10-14)

Light shines in the darkness; the Word became flesh. The One who once shouted, "Let there be light!" came to us in Jesus. This is Incarnation! The Word—the creative power and wisdom of God that spoke all things into existence—took on flesh as an infant in Bethlehem. These words are meant to inspire awe. Far more than the birth of a baby, Christmas is about the God who created and sustains the universe breaking into our world—light and life, word and flesh, grace and truth, the glory of a father's only son.

Far more than the birth of a baby, Christmas is about the God who created and sustains the universe breaking into our world— light and life, word and flesh, grace and truth, the glory of a father's only son.

Darkness and Light in Scripture

The twin ideas of darkness and light permeate the Bible. In fact, we find them on the very first page of scripture, in the first chapter of Genesis:

> *In the beginning when God created the heavens and the earth, the earth was a formless void and darkness covered the face of the deep, while a wind from God swept over the face of the waters. Then God said, "Let there be light"; and there*

was light. And God saw that the light was good;
and God separated the light from the darkness.
God called the light Day, and the darkness he
called Night.

(Genesis 1:1-5a)

We find them again on the very last page of
scripture, in Revelation 22:5: "And there will be no
more night; they need no light of lamp or sun, for
the Lord God will be their light."

The Bible's beginning and ending highlight the
tension between darkness and light, with the power
of the light coming from God. Stories of light and
darkness act as bookends in scripture.

Darkness is most often (but not always) associated with evil, adversity, ignorance, despair,
gloom, and even death. Light, on the other hand, is
usually associated in scripture with God, goodness,
joy, knowledge, hope, and life.

As an example, the writer of Proverbs noted: "The
way of the wicked is like deep darkness" (Proverbs
4:19). The writer of 1 John wrote something
similar: "But whoever hates another believer is in
the darkness, walks in the darkness, and does not
know the way to go" (1 John 2:11a). Jesus himself

sometimes described hell, a place reserved for those who choose to separate themselves from God, as "outer darkness" (Matthew 22:13).

There are two broad categories of existential darkness in scripture. The first is moral darkness; the second is what we might call situational, relational, or emotional darkness.

We know the moral darkness; we see it is all around us. We see it in terrorist attacks and mass shootings, in selfish acts that harm others. We feel it in circumstances that leave us hopeless. I think of the funerals I've done for those who took their own lives, unable to see the light for all the darkness in their world. There is the darkness we're drawn to participate in when we're tempted to do things that will harm others. I think of the abuse of children that happened at the hands of religious leaders. They sought to represent the light, but yielded to the darkness; in their darkness, they brought harm and deep darkness to others.

In chapter two, we talked about the good path we're intended to walk. That path is described in scripture as "walking in the light." When we stray from the path, we move toward the darkness. When we succumb to thoughts, words, or deeds that bring momentary gratification followed by guilt, hurt, and shame, we walk in the darkness. The battle between good and evil, light and darkness, is one of the major themes in human existence, captured in history, literature, the arts, and life. The perennial battle that defines us as human beings is the battle between good and evil, light and darkness. It is not only a battle outside of us, it is a battle that is fought *within* us.

There is a second kind of darkness found throughout scripture. It is not a moral darkness (though it is sometimes the result of bad decisions or the evil actions of others). This existential or situational darkness is associated with grief, sadness, or despair, or the feelings of being lost or unloved. Scripture speaks regularly of this type of darkness. A prime example of this is Job. A quarter of the occurrences of the word *dark* or *darkness* in the Old Testament appear in the Book of Job, including this description of Job's afflictions: "My face is red with weeping, and deep darkness is on my eyelids" (Job 16:16). The psalmist speaks of the Jewish exiles who "sat in darkness and in gloom, prisoners in misery and in irons" (Psalm 107:10).

We still use the word in this way today. Daphne Merkin, writing in *The New York Times Magazine*, described her battle with depression as a "journey through darkness."[6] Following a worship service in our chapel one Sunday, a woman in our congregation told me, "I'm feeling overwhelmed by darkness right now." Another member who lost his spouse described the grief he was feeling as "deep darkness." We know what that means because we have all been there, in that darkness.

Christmas, the Incarnation of God, is God's response to both forms of darkness, the moral and the existential.

The psalmist noted, "It is you who light my lamp; the LORD, my God, lights up my darkness" (Psalm 18:28). The prophet Micah said it this way: "Do not rejoice over me, O my enemy; when I fall, I shall rise; when I sit in darkness, the LORD will be a light to me" (Micah 7:8). David wrote, "The LORD is my light and my salvation; whom shall I fear?" (Psalm 27:1). For the believers of the Hebrew Bible, the Old Testament, it was their faith in God that brought them hope that they would make it through the darkest of times. It was their trust in the grace of God that led them to believe that no matter how far they had wandered from God, no matter how great their sin, God could and would forgive and heal them. It was their belief that God was always with them, as near as the air we breathe, and their knowledge of God's presence that helped them survive the inevitable moments of despair. They trusted, bare-knuckled, holding fast onto their faith that God was walking with them, and that God would sustain them because God is light and calls us out of darkness and chaos.

Light Incarnate—What Happened at Christmas

This takes us back to John's telling of the Christmas story, which is rooted in the Creation story and aims to make clear the cosmic significance of Jesus's Incarnation as God's response to both moral and existential darkness. John begins with the familiar words of Genesis 1:1, "In the beginning..." In Genesis 1, God creates all that is by speaking: "Then God *said*..." As God speaks, everything comes to be. In John 1, Jesus is described as the Word and, as John says, "All things came into being through him, and without him not one thing came into being." Just as God spoke in Genesis 1 and light was created, in

John 1 we read, "What has come into being in him was life, and the life was the light of all people. The light shines in the darkness, and the darkness did not overcome it."

Matthew captures the same idea, though he associates it with Jesus's ministry, when he quotes Isaiah 9: "the people who sat in darkness have seen a great light, and for those who sat in the region and shadow of death light has dawned" (Matthew 4:16).

Each week of Advent, the church lights another candle in the Advent wreath. The closer we come to Christmas, the greater the light until finally on Christmas Eve (or Christmas Day) the Christ candle is lit; the Light of the world has been born!

The angels proclaimed to the shepherds that Jesus's birth is good news of great joy for all people. God has come to us, to show us who God *is*, to remind us that he walks with us in our darkest hours, and to call us to walk in the light of his love. He came to embody the light that God brings to us—to demonstrate God's compassion to the sick, to offer God's mercy to sinners, and to teach us by his words and example how to live as children of the light. And then, in his death, he gave himself for us, demonstrating God's self-giving love; by his resurrection, he pierced the darkness of death and grief, bringing humanity the light of hope and the promise that, as Frederick Buechner has said, "the worst thing is never the last thing."

Christmas is the celebration of light piercing our darkness, God's light coming to us to enlighten our lives.

Later in his Gospel, John records that Jesus said to his disciples, "I am the light of the world. Whoever follows me will never walk in darkness but will have the light of life" (John 8:12). Still later in the same Gospel, Jesus says, "Those who walk during the day do not stumble, because they see the light of this world. But those who walk at night stumble, because the light is not in them." (John 11: 9b-10). This is the point of Christmas. It is the celebration of light piercing our darkness, God's light coming to us to enlighten our lives. We need not fear that we will stumble or become lost because we are no longer trying to find our way in the dark; we have the light of Christ by which we walk.

Many Christians are unaware that the reason we celebrate Christmas on December 25 relates to this interplay between light and darkness, and the coming of Jesus as the Light of the world. No one knows the precise day when Jesus was born. In the first century, Jewish people did not typically celebrate birthdays. Parents did not obtain government-issued certificates that recorded the date of a child's birth.

Early Christians focused more on the death and resurrection of Jesus. Those events could be dated because they were connected to Passover, and dates for Passover can be calculated using a lunar calendar. As long as the Crucifixion and Resurrection were the emphasis, the date of Jesus's birth was anyone's guess. But over time, there was a yearning to celebrate Jesus's birth as well, not simply to commemorate his birthday, but as a way of celebrating the Incarnation—the moment when God entered our world, when the light came to push back the darkness.

Not knowing the day when Christ was born, one day seemed most fitting: the winter solstice. In the northern hemisphere, the winter solstice occurred on December 25 according to the Julian calendar (the calendar of the Roman Empire and the West until at least the sixteenth century AD). Today, we use the Gregorian calendar, and the winter solstice usually occurs on December 21 (and the 22 every fourth year). Why did early Christians choose to celebrate Christ's birth on the winter solstice? Some would say it was to replace the pagan festivals as the empire was Christianized. It is true that people throughout history have celebrated the winter solstice with festivals. But I believe the real reason is that on this day, the heavens themselves proclaimed Christmas and the significance of the Incarnation. Up until the winter solstice, darkness and night increase for months, and daytime and light recede. But the winter solstice marks the turning point, where the heavens themselves declare that light has conquered the darkness. Light triumphs over darkness; daytime pushes back the night. "The light shines in the darkness and the darkness did not overcome it."

God came to us, as one of us, to bring light into our darkness. He came to save us from ourselves—from our tendency to succumb to the darkness—to call us to walk in the light and to take his light into the world. And he came to save us from the existential darkness that at times overwhelms us. He came to show that he walks with us through the dark, scary places in our lives, even through "the darkest valley" or as the King James Version has it, "the valley of the shadow of death" (Psalm 23:4).

The Word of God

Before exploring further this idea of Christ as the Light of the world, I'd like to spend a moment lingering on the other title John uses to describe Jesus in his account of the Incarnation. Once more we read:

> In the beginning was the Word, and the Word was with God, and the Word was God....
>
> And the Word became flesh and lived among us.

What an odd name or title for Jesus: *the Word*. In Greek, it is *logos*, which means "word," but also has the connotation of reasoning, wisdom, or logic. In fact, our word *logic* comes from *logos*. You see the word *logos* in many English words that end in *ology*—biology, zoology, psychology—fields which represent the wisdom, reasoning, and authority about bio, zoo, psyche.

Jesus is the Incarnation, the authoritative Word, wisdom, and reasoning about God. While Christians often speak about the Bible as the Word of God, the Word of God in its most decisive and definitive form came to us not as a book, but as a person. Jesus is God's self-disclosure, God's revelation of himself to humanity. God's Word was incarnate in Jesus. All other words about God, everything else we read in scripture, must be read in the light of the Word of God that is Jesus. He incarnates the wisdom, reasoning, mind, and heart of God.

This Word of God, this Light of the world, came to us as a baby. What an odd way for God to speak his definitive word to us. But it made sense to me after I had my own children. LaVon and I were fortunate to be able to have children and we chose to do so out of a deep desire to give love away.

Every year on the eve of their birthdays, since each daughter was born, I have written a letter to them. In that letter, I described how much I loved them, my hopes and dreams for them, and I summarized the events that had happened in the previous year. I'd never been sure that these letters meant much to them. When they were young,

I would read the letters to them. As they got older, I would give them to them to read on their own.

I wondered when I'd stop writing these letters. For my oldest daughter, I decided that would be her twenty-eighth birthday. Nine months earlier, she had given birth to her own daughter. That year, for her birthday, I bound together all of her birthday letters since the first one, the one I wrote the night before her birth. I gave her this collection of letters, saying, "Danielle, I was never sure when to stop writing. I have always wanted you to know how much you were loved. I realized this year, I could stop writing. You now have a daughter of your own and you now know just how much a parent loves a child. You know how much I love you."

It was then that it occurred to me that this was something of what John had in mind when he called Jesus *the Word*. Jesus was God's Word, God's testament to his love for us. These letters I wrote were not all that revealed my love to my daughter. In fact, I hoped they just testified to the love she'd seen, felt, and experienced from me all her life. In the same way, Jesus's words, actions, suffering, death, and resurrection embodied and incarnated the light of God's love for the world, the love that has been there all along in other ways too. I think this is what John meant when he wrote, "For God so loved the world that he gave his only Son" (John 3:16). In a sense, John was saying that Jesus is God's love letter to his children.

Walking in and Sharing the Light

Jesus is God's Word to us. In that Word, we see not only the love of God, but the light of God illuminating our moral and existential darkness. Our task is to accept that light, to allow it to illuminate our lives, to walk in this light, and to then share this light with others.

It's not surprising that some have spoken of their conversion as a moment when they "saw the light." This was certainly how the early church understood conversion. It was a leaving behind of darkness and living in and expressing Christ's light. As Peter wrote to his readers: "[God] called you out of darkness into his marvelous light" (1 Peter 2:9). Paul, whose own conversion experience involved a brilliant, blinding light, wrote to the Ephesian Christians: "For once you were darkness, but now in the Lord you are light. Live as children of light—for the fruit of the light is found in all that is good and right and true"

(Ephesians 5:8-9). Centuries later, John Newton, drawing from the stories of Jesus opening the eyes of the blind, would describe his conversion from darkness to light by saying, "I once was lost, but now am found, was blind, but now I see." When we say yes to Jesus, when we yield our lives to him, we move from darkness into light.

When we say yes to Jesus, when we yield our lives to him, we move from darkness into light.

In John's Gospel, Jesus told his disciples, "I am the light of the world" (John 8:12). But I love how in Matthew's Gospel, Jesus turns to his disciples and says, "You are the light of the world. A city built on a hill cannot be hid....Let your light shine before others, so that they may see your good works and give glory to your Father in heaven" (Matthew 5:14, 16). He is the light, and as we come to him, trust in him, and begin to follow him, we walk in his light. We bear his light within us or, as we considered in the last chapter, we incarnate his light.

Returning to the candlelight service on Christmas Eve, it is these two movements that we capture in the candle-lighting: the movement to accept Christ's light and the movement to reflect his light. Everyone receives a small, unlit candle as they walk into our Christmas Eve service. After the lights are dimmed and the Advent candles extinguished, after John's telling of the Christmas story from John 1 is read, we light the Christ candle. Then we remember that Jesus grew up to be a man. He taught about God's kingdom, he healed the sick, he cast out demons, he forgave sinners. He drove out the darkness, and ultimately, he suffered and died as an expression of God's selfless love and grace. And then, on the third day, he rose from the grave, conquering evil, hate, sin, and death. Light triumphed over darkness.

Then I remind the congregation, as I light my candle, that Jesus not only said, "I am the light of the world," but he also said, "You are the light of the world." Here he used the plural you—together.

"So," I tell the congregation, "at Christmas we celebrate that God came to us in Jesus, bringing his light to the world. But we are meant to accept that light. John tells us, 'But to all who received him, who believed in his name, he gave power to become children of God' (John 1:12). In a moment, we'll pass the candlelight from person to person. When you light your candle, pause to pray, 'Lord, I need your light. I accept your light and love.'" Then we invite them to share their lights with their neighbors.

We sing "Silent Night, Holy Night" as we pass the candlelight, filling the room. And then, after all the candles are lit, I say to the congregation, "This is beautiful, all of you together, your faces bathed in candlelight. Now hold up your light." They all hold up their candles and the room is filled with light. It is breathtaking. And then I say, "This was God's big idea in sending Jesus. A moment ago, one small candle entered this room of darkness. A very small light for such a dark place. But God's strategy was that those who believed in Jesus, who received his name, would have his light within them. And they would then reflect his light and live his light in acts of justice, mercy, and love. In this way, through *us*, each of us doing our part to push back the darkness, the world would be filled with light. This is the mission, the calling, the vision, and the promise of Christmas!"

God knows the darkness in our world. God knows there are tens of thousands of children in this country who go to bed hungry most every night. God sees the millions who have no bed of their own because they have no place to call home. God sees the evil that people do to one another and how that evil causes injury and pain. And sometimes we may be tempted to ask why God allows so much suffering and injustice. Why didn't God do anything to stop it?

Here is God's answer: "I did do something. I sent Jesus to be the light so you could see what to do. He came to bring good news to the poor, to set the prisoners free, and to unfasten every yoke that burdens your fellow children and holds them down. He came that you might walk in his light and that you might incarnate his love, light, and justice for the world."

---

*We are God's plan
for changing the world....
We are not just passive
recipients of God's love and grace.*

We are God's plan for changing the world. Let that soak in. We are God's strategic plan for addressing poverty. We are God's plan for addressing injustice, for healing the wounds of injury and suffering. We are God's plan for including every person in this beloved community. We are not just passive recipients of God's love and grace. As we become children of the light, we cannot keep that light within ourselves. It is meant to spill out from us naturally and touch the lives of others. And every time it does, the light extends just a little farther, the darkness recedes bit by bit, the kingdom of God expands, and the world is changed.

God sent Jesus to launch a revolution of the heart that ultimately leads us to take his light into the world. And how do we do that? It starts with watchfulness—paying attention to see where someone needs our support or our assistance. It starts with saying to God: "Here I am. Use me to take your light into the dark places." And then we carry that light through acts of selfless love. In his first epistle John writes, "…the darkness is passing away and the true light is already shining. Whoever says, 'I am in the light,' while hating a brother or sister, is still in the darkness. Whoever loves a brother or sister lives in the light" (1 John 2:8b-10a).

What does carrying light into the dark places look like? Centuries before Jesus, Isaiah the prophet pointed the people of Israel toward an answer when he wrote, "If you offer your food to the hungry and satisfy the needs of the afflicted, then your light shall rise in the darkness and your gloom be like the noonday" (Isaiah 58:10). When you loosen the bonds of injustice, share your bread with the hungry, and provide shelter for the homeless and clothes for those who lack them, God declares, "then your light shall break forth like the dawn, and your healing shall spring up quickly" (Isaiah 58:8).

I love Isaiah's vision. When you care for someone in need; when you bless and encourage someone; when you feed them and provide beds for others if they sleep on the floor; when you give someone who has no education the chance to go to school—your light will break forth like the dawn, pushing away the darkness. Your healing will spring up quickly; when you help heal the hurt and brokenness in others, you receive healing too. Your gloom will be like the noonday.

When you do good for others, you do good for yourself. Love that gives of itself is better than a pill. It heals you. When you take your eyes off yourself and focus on others, realizing that it's not about you, then you find joy and fulfillment. When you share the light, you also receive it.

A parishioner I know has struggled with depression most of her life. She's been on a variety of antidepressants and seen a variety of psychiatrists and therapists. These all have played a part in her healing. But recently she told me that the most healing thing she does is serving low-income children, both in Kansas City and in Africa. When she talks about this, her face lights up. As St. Francis of Assisi said, "It is in giving that we receive."

Several years ago, reporter Steve Hartman on the *CBS News* highlighted the story of a wealthy businessman who began taking on the role of Secret Santa to people in Kansas City. The man, who insisted on remaining anonymous, gave away $100,000 during the Christmas season. He did it $100 at a time, randomly giving a crisp new bill to people he saw for whom he thought the extra money could make a difference.

As the news story on CBS explained, in 2014 the man "deputized" officers in the county sheriff's office to help him with his giveaway. The deputies would stop people who seemed deserving, who then were both shocked and overjoyed to learn that they were receiving this gift out of the blue. One young mother began to cry; she hadn't been able to afford Christmas gifts for her children, but now they could have presents waiting for them on Christmas morning. Especially in a time when so many communities were experiencing tension between residents and the police, the deputies were gratified to be able to spread joy to others—and to receive hugs from people they had helped. Those small acts of community healing were part of the anonymous businessman's design in the aftermath of events in Ferguson, Missouri, that year. That 2014 story quickly went viral and was seen by more than forty million people. Hartman has returned to Kansas City in subsequent Christmas seasons to air updates.[7]

After I saw that first story, I was curious about what motivated this Secret Santa to do what he did. I thought that someone from Church of the Resurrection might know his identity, so I sent out a message on our Facebook page. Sure enough, someone knew him and passed along the message that I'd like to talk with him. Shortly after that, I received a call on my cell phone from the man (with his caller ID blocked, naturally).

I had lots of questions. "Why are you doing this?" I asked him. "What makes you tick? Why have you traveled across the country and recruited other Secret Santas to do the same thing in other cities?"

He told me, "I'm trying to show God's love for those who are down on their luck. The money is just an expression of unconditional love. Kindness is a bridge that crosses all races and denominations. The act of giving kindness brings joy not only to the recipient, but to the giver as well."

He wanted to bring joy both to those who received the money and to the sheriffs who were distributing it. He understood that the joy is multiplied when you're bringing it to others, not just receiving it. You could see it in the faces of the deputies as they went about this work of pushing darkness away with light.

"By the way, Pastor," added Secret Santa (I never learned his actual name), "the first Secret Santas were the wise men, you know. They traveled a long distance to go help a homeless family and to honor the Christ Child with their gifts of gold, frankincense, and myrrh. And they did it anonymously too." He was right. In Matthew's Gospel, the magi are anonymous; it wasn't until hundreds of years later that the church gave names to them. They did not come to Bethlehem seeking recognition, but only to bless, help, and honor the one who received their gifts.

In our world, you're either bringing darkness or light. By your words and deeds, you bring joy, love, and hope to others or you take it away. You bless and build up or you tear down and hurt. Life is either all about you or it is about others.

In our world, you're either bringing darkness or light. By your words and deeds, you bring joy, love, and hope to others or you take it away. You bless and build up or you tear down and hurt. Life is either all about you or it is about others.

We have a tradition on Christmas Eve services at Church of the Resurrection. Many other congregations have a similar tradition. The families who light the Christ candle each year are families who experienced darkness that year, but turned to Christ to be their light. They've lost jobs, or had been through a critical illness, or lost a loved one. I usually don't know which families are doing it until they approach to light the Christ candle.

Several years ago, I looked up and found myself moved to tears as I saw the family ascending the steps to the Christ candle. Eight months earlier, two members of their family had been murdered in a terrible hate crime intended to terrorize and kill members of the Jewish community. These two members of our congregation were at the Jewish community center for a talent show, a grandfather taking his grandson for tryouts. The double funeral was held during Holy Week. Still picking up the pieces of their lives, the surviving family members stood in the darkness of the sanctuary, holding one small candle with which to light the Christ candle.

No one else could see their faces. The congregation didn't know who was lighting the candle. But for me, this moment captured the meaning of Christmas. They had suffered the terrible impact of moral darkness and they knew the agony of existential darkness. This was their hope for healing: that this story, captured by their act of lighting the Christ candle, was really true; light came into the darkness and the darkness could not overcome it.

Jesus is the Word of God incarnate—God's desire to be known, to speak to us, to be heard by us, made flesh. And he is the Light of the world. May you hear this word, accept his light, and reflect his light this Christmas.

Jesus, I trust in you. Be my light. Fill me with your light. Grant me your hope. Help me to walk in your light, to share your light, to live your light, to give your light. Use me, I pray, to push back the darkness. In your holy name. Amen.

EPILOGUE

EPIPHANY...
FALLING TO
OUR KNEES

In the time of King Herod, after Jesus was born in Bethlehem of Judea, wise men from the East came to Jerusalem, asking "Where is the child who has been born king of the Jews? We observed his star at its rising, and have come to pay him homage."...

Then he sent them to Bethlehem.... When they had heard the king, they set out; and there, ahead of them, went the star that they had seen at its rising, until it stopped over the place where the child was. When they saw that the star had stopped, they were overwhelmed with joy. On entering the house, they saw the child with Mary his mother; and they knelt down and paid him homage. Then, opening their treasure chests, they offered him gifts of gold, frankincense, and myrrh.

(Matthew 2:1-2, 8a, 9-11)

If you've been reading this book for Advent, and you've read one chapter a week, then you've arrived at this final chapter on Christmas Day (or more likely a day or two after). We lit our candles on Christmas Eve, opened our stockings and gifts on Christmas morning, and celebrated the birth of Jesus with friends, family, and more food than we should have eaten. Now, it's time to pack up our decorations, put away our Nativity sets, toss the Christmas cards, and store or discard our tree for another year. Advent and Christmas are over; it's on to the new year, right?

The answer to this is *no* on two scores. First, Matthew and Luke offer us several more stories, what are typically called the "infancy narratives," before they leave behind the Christmas themes. These include the visit of the magi, the circumcision and dedication of Jesus at the temple where the elderly Anna and Simeon bless Jesus, and the Holy Family's flight to Egypt as Herod seeks to kill the newborn King. We'll touch on these stories briefly in this chapter.

Advent and Christmas are only the beginning of the story, not the end. Their messages are meant to shape us all year long.

But there's a second, deeper sense in which Advent and Christmas cannot be over. Advent and Christmas are only the beginning of the story, not the end. Their messages are meant to shape us all year long. It is this point we'll conclude with as we look at one final title for Jesus that the Christmas stories first reveal. But first, let's briefly explore the infancy narratives of Luke and Matthew.

The Dedication of Jesus at the Temple

In Luke's infancy narratives, Mary, Joseph, and Jesus remain (presumably) in Bethlehem for forty-one days after Jesus's birth. We're told about two events that take place during this time. On the eighth day after his birth, Jesus was circumcised, likely at the home where he was staying. This was in fulfillment of God's command to Abraham in Genesis 17:12, a command followed dutifully by observant Jews then as now.

Thirty-three days after a child's circumcision, the Law of Moses commanded that the child be dedicated to God and that a sacrifice be offered for his mother's purification. A lamb and a dove were to be offered, but if one was poor, two pigeons were accepted instead. Luke tells us that Mary and Joseph offered two pigeons, another reminder of the economic status of the Holy Family (see Leviticus 12:1-8). This took place at the temple.

As they entered the temple courts, a devout and faithful man named Simeon, whom the Spirit led to the temple that day, saw the Holy Family. He approached and took Jesus in his arms. Then he prayed to God saying,

> *"Master, now you are dismissing your*
> *servant in peace,*
> *according to your word;*
> *for my eyes have seen your salvation,*

> *which you have prepared in the presence*
> *of all peoples,*
> *a light for revelation to the Gentiles*
> *and for glory to your people Israel."*
> *(Luke 2:29-32)*

Notice that in Simeon's prophetic prayer, he speaks of two of the four themes we've covered in previous chapters: Jesus as the source of God's salvation, and Jesus as a light for revelation. But Simeon doesn't stop there. He goes on to say to Mary, "This boy is destined for the falling and the rising of many in Israel, and to be a sign that will be opposed so that the inner thoughts of many will be revealed—and a sword will pierce your own soul too" (Luke 2:24). In this infancy narrative, we learn that Jesus, and the response of people to him, will reveal the innermost thoughts—the motivations—of many, and that Jesus's life will end in opposition and ultimately in grief for his mother. A grief the reader knows will come from his crucifixion.

This is a reminder that the Christmas story is only the beginning. It is always pointing us toward the rest of Jesus's story: his life, teachings, ministry, death, and resurrection. Among the most meaningful Christmas ornaments I've ever had was one given me by my Uncle Glenn. It was a long nail with a ribbon by which to hang it at the top. The nail was to go near the trunk of the tree, a reminder that the child whose birth we celebrate would one day be nailed to the timbers from a tree. There should always be a recognition, as we celebrate Christmas, that this child is destined to die for us.

Shortly after Simeon speaks to Mary, an 84-year-old widow named Anna, a prophet, came and "began to praise God and to speak about the child to all who were looking forward to the redemption of Jerusalem" (Luke 2:38). Redemption once more reminds us of something we spoke of in a previous chapter. It was a word used to describe the payment made to free a slave or someone who was imprisoned due to debt. It was to purchase back or to regain the freedom of another. Paul noted, "You were bought with a price" (1 Corinthians 6:20) and we remember how Bonhoeffer powerfully described the costliness of God's grace. Anna reminds us of these things. Christmas will climax in our redemption. Shortly after these dramatic encounters with Simeon and Anna, according to Luke's Gospel, Joseph and Mary take Jesus to Nazareth.

The Visit of the Magi

Matthew tells us nothing about the circumcision or dedication. Instead, he focuses on two different stories he feels are essential to tell. Both stories are closely associated with themes of Matthew's Gospel. The first is the coming of the magi, the wise men from the East. The second is the flight to Egypt, where Joseph takes Mary and Jesus as King Herod seeks to kill the child.

The first story, the coming of the magi, makes it clear right from the start that Christmas—and the redemption and salvation Christ brings—is not just for the Jewish people, but for *everyone*. By the end of the Gospel, Matthew will make this crystal clear as Jesus gives his disciples the Great Commission, telling them to "go therefore and make disciples of *all* nations" (Matthew 28:19, emphasis added). Let's consider briefly the coming of the magi.

Matthew reports, "In the time of King Herod, after Jesus was born in Bethlehem of Judea, wise men from the East came to Jerusalem, asking 'Where is the child who has been born king of the Jews? We observed his star at its rising, and have come to pay him homage'" (Matthew 2:1-2). Magi—from which we have our word *magician*—were from Persia

155

(modern-day Iran) and were a caste of priests of the Zoroastrian religion (which shared some theological ideas with Judaism). The magi studied the stars, believing that they foretold events on earth; today we would call them astrologers. While astrology is not commended in the Bible, God spoke to these magi in the way they were seeking—through the stars.

In Luke's Gospel, it is the night-shift shepherds who are the first to learn that the Messiah has been born. But in Matthew, it is the wealthy foreigners, truth-seekers of another religion from a faraway land, that God first beckons to see the newborn King. Luke and Matthew complement each other well here. Jesus came for rich and poor, for the uneducated and those who had spent their lives studying. He came for the Jews and also for the people of other faiths who were earnestly seeking the truth. These magi are the first of many Gentiles—non-Jews—who will kneel at the feet of Jesus to honor him.

There are several Persian families who worship with us at Resurrection. Most were raised Muslim but were drawn to our church by a ministry, program, or by the witness of their friends who invited them to attend. They are beautiful people. Regardless of their faith background, people of Persia all know this story. They also know of Zoroastrianism, which still has about thirty thousand adherents in Iran. There is an excitement as we discuss this story together and when I, as a pastor, recognize what they already know—that the first people to pay homage to Jesus, at least in Matthew's Gospel, were Persian wise men. When I speak to my Persian parishioners, I'm reminded of God's love for the magi.

These magi traveled across the ancient highways of the Fertile Crescent, a route of some twelve hundred miles that would have taken a caravan at least a hundred days to cross. They would have traveled another hundred days back home. This journey would have come at no small personal cost. They were determined to honor this newborn King. They came believing the stars were telling the birth of the long-awaited Jewish Messiah.

Zoroastrians believed in a messiah, a figure they called the *Saoshyant*, one who would restore the world. Did they believe this newborn King of the Jews might be their long-awaited Messiah too? We cannot know. We do know that this story tells us of God's deep concern for these magi who, though of another faith, were honored by God with the invitation to be among the first to meet the newborn king.

I love what this story says about the wideness of God's mercy. The Zoroastrians may have shared things in common with the Jews, but many of their theological views were quite different. Yet God, in his mercy, saw the earnestness of their faith, beckoned them, and blessed them. He then used them to care for the infant Jesus, bringing to him gifts of gold, frankincense, and myrrh. These gifts may be Matthew's clue to readers that, from the start, Jesus was fulfilling the words of Isaiah 60:1-6, which begins with the words, "Arise, shine; for your light has come, and the glory of the Lord has risen upon you," and ends promising that people would come from the ends of the earth to Jerusalem as God's light was revealed to them. When they did, they would bring gifts including "gold and frankincense."

Others have seen in these gifts a prophetic picture of Jesus's identity and destiny: gold, the gift offered to a king; frankincense, the gift offered by the priests to God; and myrrh, used in burial and pointing toward Christ's death. Matthew does not spell this out, and it seems likely that his primary reference in mentioning these gifts is to point to Isaiah's words that all people would be drawn to God's light, just as these magi had been drawn to Jesus.

Upon seeing the infant Jesus, these magi fall to their knees and pay him homage. Remember this, because we'll come back to it in a moment.

The Flight to Egypt: Emmanuel

Shortly after the magi leave, Joseph is forced to take Mary and Jesus and flee to Egypt. King Herod, having heard of the magi's quest to meet the child "born king of the Jews," determined to kill the child, whom he saw as a threat to his dynasty. The story, though not mentioned outside of Matthew 2, is consistent with what we know of Herod. He was paranoid, power hungry, and willing to kill even his own wife and children when he felt they might usurp his power. The Holy Family is forced to flee for their lives, becoming refugees in Egypt.

We live in a world where tens of millions of people have been forced to flee from their homes and villages due to famine, political unrest, violence, religious persecution, and war. Today, we see families with small children fleeing violence in Central American countries and seeking to enter America from the south. Visit certain African nations and you'll find families with small children fleeing religious violence in their countries. In Lebanon and

Turkey (and a host of other countries) are millions of displaced children from Syria. This is just to name a few places where the refugee crisis is felt today. I've visited Bethlehem on many occasions. It is a West Bank city, part of the Palestinian-controlled territory. Every Palestinian Christian I've ever spoken to identifies with Jesus's flight to Egypt and his refugee status there, as most see themselves as refugees.

To every refugee family, whether they are Christians or not, the fact that Jesus and his family were forced to flee political violence at the hands of a dictator and to live for a time in a country that was not their own is deeply moving. Emmanuel, God among us, experienced life as a refugee.

Epiphany: the Light of Christ Revealed

Thirteen days after Christmas comes the feast or celebration of Epiphany. For Christians in the West, Epiphany is January 6. The word itself means *to appear* or *to be seen* or *manifest*. Epiphany represents God revealing his light and presence through Jesus to the world, with a particular emphasis on the Gentile world. The story of the magi is the archetypal story of God beckoning Gentiles to himself. On

Epiphany, Christians also remember the story of Jesus's baptism at the age of thirty, during which the Spirit descended upon Jesus as a dove. God the Father spoke from heaven saying, "This is my Son, the Beloved; listen to him!" (Mark 9:7).

"I am bringing you good news
of great joy for all the people: to
you is born this day in the city
of David a Savior, who is the
Messiah, the Lord."
(Luke 2:10-11)

The magi bowing before the infant Christ, and the voice of the Father announcing that Jesus is his beloved Son, calling us to "listen to him," leads to one final word given in the Christmas story that I'd end our study with. This title was the essential affirmation of early Christians, so that Paul could say that if an individual professed this of Jesus, and believed in Christ's resurrection, they were saved. It is this title that captures the essential relationship Christians have with Jesus. What is that word?

Listen again to the words of the angel to the night-shift shepherds that first Christmas: "I am bringing you good news of great joy for all the people: to you is born this day in the city of David a Savior, who is the Messiah, *the Lord*" (Luke 2:10-11, italics added).

He is the *Lord, but is He* Your *Lord?*

No other title is used more frequently for Jesus by the early church, and in the New Testament, than *Lord*. It appears over six hundred times in the New Testament with reference to Jesus (and over a hundred other times more broadly to refer to God, and at times simply as a title of respect addressing individuals). The earliest Christian creed was simply the phrase, "Jesus is Lord." Paul writes in Romans 10:9, "If you confess with your lips that Jesus is Lord and believe in your heart that God raised him from the dead, you will be saved." And in 1 Corinthians 12:3 he writes, "No one can say 'Jesus is Lord' except by the Holy Spirit."

The word *Lord*, like most of the other words or titles we've studied, is not one in common usage today. It was a common title in the ancient world, but today has lost its meaning in part because it is now used almost exclusively of Jesus, and hence its everyday meaning is obscured to us.

The English word *lord* signifies someone in authority, typically the highest person in authority in a given realm—whether in the house, the community, or the nation. It comes from the Old English *hlaford* or *hlafweard*—loaf-warden, eventually shortened to lo-ard and then lord. It meant the "keeper of the loaf," the person who protected and held authority to determine the distribution of the bread or the resources of the family, community, or realm. The loaf-warden was the title of the person "in charge." By the way, the term *lady* comes from the Old English *hladige*, which meant loaf-kneader, the person who made the bread. In the patriarchal world of the past, *lord* and *lady* were terms that described authority and function in a home or community.

The head of the household is still called *lord* in some English-speaking countries. In England, a city's mayor is still called the Lord Mayor and the upper house of Parliament is the House of Lords. All of which might start to help us understand the significance of this title for Jesus, whom the writer of Revelation referred to as "Lord of lords."

The Greek word *lord*, translated by the English, is *kyrios*. It, too, was used as an honorific term of respect, similar to the English *sir*, but was also the common Greek word used to address the head of the house, a master or owner by employees or slaves. Like the English use of the word, it was a title used of the highest authority in a given realm: the governor, the king. The king of all earthly kings, at least within the Roman Empire, was the emperor of Rome.

The people of the Empire were to give their highest allegiance to the emperor. He was *kyrios*, or in Latin, *dominus* (from which we have the word *dominate*). He was also known as *imperator* (from which we have the word *emperor*), a word that means "to command." *Augustus* meant majestic. *Princeps* was another imperial title meaning "first," "primary," or "leader." *Pontifex maximus* was used of the emperor—it meant "high priest" who interceded with the gods. Roman coins often included the title *divi f*, short for *divi fillius*, which meant son of a god (Julius Caesar was deified by the Roman Senate upon his death—as if the Roman Senate could make their deceased rulers divine by decree!). As earthly powers went, Augustus, and the emperors that followed him, was not merely a lord; he was *the Lord*.

It is no accident that Luke begins his telling of the Christmas story by saying, "In those days Caesar Augustus..." (Luke 2:1 CEB). It would seem that Luke wants us to make the connection and to see the contrast between Caesar and Christ. Caesar commands a census that forces the Holy Family to travel to Bethlehem. Mary gives birth in a stable among the animals—essentially homeless—with an animal's feeding trough as Jesus's bed. This is as humble and lowly a birth as one can imagine in the first century. In the Empire, Caesar is "Lord." But the angel came announcing to the night-shift shepherds, as we've read already, "I am bringing you good news of great joy for all the people: to you is born this day in the city of David a Savior, who is the Messiah, *the Lord*" (emphasis added).

We've learned that the word *messiah* means "anointed one" and is essentially another word for *king*. This child whose birth the angels announced was both king and lord. But he is not just *a* lord. He is not simply a local king serving under the auspices of the emperor as King Herod was. The angels were announcing that Jesus was *the* Lord, or as Revelation describes him, "Lord of lords and King of kings" (Revelation 17:14 and 19:16).

As the early Christians said, "Jesus is Lord," they were saying several things. They were saying, "Jesus is the highest authority in my life. He is my Master, Sovereign, Ruler, Commander, and King." *Lord* was not simply a name they used to addressed Jesus; it was a title that reflected their submission to his will. When we begin our prayers, "Lord…" we are acknowledging his authority in our lives. We are yielding our lives, our hearts, and our wills to his will.

The first Christians were clear that Jesus was the Lord, not Caesar. Christmas's celebration comes just days before a new Congress is sworn in every other year, and less than a month before Inauguration Day every four years. It is a good time to recall that regardless of our political affiliation—or whether our candidate or party won or lost—Jesus is Lord. It is to him we give our highest allegiance.

I'd like to invite you to consider this when you pray. When you address Jesus as Lord, you are acknowledging his authority. You are recognizing that you belong to him. You are expressing your relationship to him. You are yielding your life to him. To be a Christian is not only to say, but to live the words *Jesus is Lord*.

To be a Christian is not only to say, but to live the words Jesus is Lord.

Finally, Paul and the earliest Christians were not unaware that in their Bible, what we call the Old Testament, the word *Lord* translates to the Hebrew word *Adonai*. Like the words *lord* and *kyrios*, it means master, ruler, sovereign. It could be used of people, but it was also a term used most often in the Old Testament as a title for or name for God. When the Jewish people stopped speaking God's personal name, *Yahweh*, they began substituting the word *Adonai* in its place. When the Hebrew Bible was translated into Greek, the word *kyrios* became the most commonly used word or title for God. This was not lost on early Christians. When they called Jesus *Lord*, they were expressing the mystery that in Jesus God had come to us; Jesus was the Incarnation of Yahweh.

Returning to the story of the magi we remember at Epiphany, the wise men knelt down as they presented their gifts of gold, frankincense, and myrrh to the Christ Child. I wake up every morning and slip to my knees next to my bed as I begin my day. I did this again this morning; I'll do it tomorrow morning, and the next, and the next, until I can no longer slip to my knees. Even then, I'll continue to do this in my heart. I seek to bow before Christ, giving thanks to him. Honoring him. Yielding my life to him.

It is this daily yielding of our lives to Christ that makes clear that Christmas is not over when the tree comes down and the decorations are packed for another year. Advent and Christmas are meant to call us to a lifelong journey of daily offering our lives to Christ, our Lord.

Our Christmas Eve candlelight service ends the same way every year. With the candles lit throughout the room, we sing. It's the same carol we end with every year as it captures the impact the Incarnation has on our lives. We sing, "Joy to the World."

> Joy to the world, the Lord is come!
> Let earth receive her King;
> let every heart prepare him room,
> and heaven and nature sing,
> and heaven and nature sing,
> and heaven, and heaven, and nature sing.
>
> Joy to the world, the Savior reigns!
> Let all their songs employ;

while fields and floods, rocks, hills, and plains
repeat the sounding joy,
repeat the sounding joy,
repeat, repeat the sounding joy.

No more let sins and sorrows grow,
nor thorns infest the ground;
he comes to make his blessings flow
far as the curse is found,
far as the curse is found,
far as, far as the curse is found.

He rules the world with truth and grace,
and makes the nations prove
the glories of his righteousness,
and wonders of his love,
and wonders of his love,
and wonders, wonders of his love.

May this joy be yours as you hail Jesus as your Christ, your Messiah, your King. May you taste of the hope and mercy he offers as you receive him as your Savior. May you feel his peace as you accept that he is your Emmanuel. May you hear him as God's definitive Word to you, even as you allow his light to dwell in you and be reflected through you. May he be your Lord; guiding, leading, and directing your path.

For the final prayer of this book, I share with you a prayer I've shared in many of my books. It's a prayer prayed by John Wesley and the early Methodists as a way of yielding their lives to Jesus as Lord, and inviting him to use them. I invite you to make this your prayer as you offer yourself to Christ, our Savior, Emmanuel, the Light of the world, the Word Made Flesh—Jesus, our Lord:

I am no longer my own, but thine.

Put me to what thou wilt, rank me with whom
  thou wilt.

Put me to doing, put me to suffering.

Let me be employed by thee or laid aside for thee,

exalted for thee or brought low for thee.

Let me be full, let me be empty.

Let me have all things, let me have nothing.

I freely and heartily yield all things to thy pleasure
  and disposal.

And now, O glorious and blessed God,

Father, Son, and Holy Spirit,

thou art mine, and I am thine. So be it.

And the covenant which I have made on earth,

let it be ratified in heaven. Amen.

ACKNOWLEDGMENTS

I am grateful to my colleagues and partners in publishing at Abingdon Press. To Susan Salley, who heads up my team at Abingdon. I'm so grateful for her support, encouragement, and friendship. To Brian Sigmon and his excellent editorial work. The mistakes and shortcomings in this book are my own, but to the degree that there is anything helpful and speaks to the reader, Brian was instrumental in making that happen. To Alan Vermilye, who does an excellent job of publicizing and sharing my books, and helping them to find their way into the hands of readers. To Tim Cobb, for his tireless work in keeping this book on schedule and assuring its quality. To Tracey Craddock, Leigh Ray, Pat Holland, Laura Lockhart, and the others at Abingdon whose contributions have made this book possible. And to the Cokesbury Team—I love you all! Thank you for your work in helping pastors and churches find excellent resources to serve the church. You amaze me.

Finally, I want to acknowledge my wife, LaVon. She is my best friend, my muse, and my partner. I write books at night, on my days off, and on vacation. This year, to complete this book and make it available for you, the reader, she sacrificed time (perhaps the most precious thing we have as we get older) in order for me to write. Countless evenings and holidays she has spent alone so that I might complete these books. LaVon, I love you. Thank you for your sacrifices—without you this book and many others would not have been possible.

NOTES

1. John Wesley, *Explanatory Notes Upon the New Testament* (London: John Mason, 1755).
2. Mark Easton, "Coronation 1953: Magic moment the TV cameras missed," BBC News, June 4, 2013, https://www.bbc.com/news/uk-22764987.
3. James S. Stewart, *King Forever* (Abingdon Press, 1975), 15.
4. Dietrich Bonhoeffer, *The Cost of Discipleship* (Touchstone, 1995), 45.
5. The Doctors: "The Ebola fighters in their own words," *Time Magazine*, December 10, 2014, https://time.com/time-person-of-the-year-ebola -doctors/.
6. Daphne Merkin, "A Journey Through Darkness," *The New York Times Magazine*, May 10, 2009, https://www.nytimes.com/2009/05/10 /magazine/10Depression-t.html.
7. Steve Hartman, "Unique traffic stops in Missouri bring drivers to tears," *CBS News*, December 12, 2014, https://www.cbsnews.com/news/sheriffs -deputies-kindness-brings-drivers-to-tears/.

A New Study of the Ten Commandments from
ADAM HAMILTON

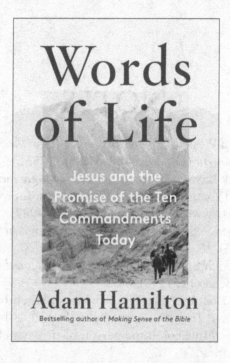

The Ten Commandments have shaped the lives of Jews and Christians for three millennia. In *Words of Life*, Adam Hamilton explores what each of the Ten Commandments meant to the ancient Israelites, how Jesus reinterpreted and lived them, and finally how these words lead us to the good life God intends for us today.

Available wherever books are sold 12.29.20

I n this six-week study based on his book *Words of Life*, Adam Hamilton brings modern eyes to the most important set of ethics in history. For churchwide Lenten study or for small groups any time, readers will consider the commandments in their historical context, consider the meaning of each commandment in Hebrew, unpack how Jesus reinterpreted them, and show how every "thou shalt not" was intended to point to a life-giving "thou shalt."

In addition to the Leader Guide, which includes session plans, activities and discussion questions, a youth leader guide, a children's leader guide, and a DVD are available. The DVD features Adam Hamilton teaching on site in Egypt and insightful conversations with Rabbi Art Nemitoff.

Available wherever fine books are sold.
For more information about Adam Hamilton, visit www.AdamHamilton.com.